—TRADITIONS OF —
TRINITY AND LEITH

REVISED AND EXTENDED

On more than one occasion the fortunes of Leith have been the point on which the whole history of our country has turned.

John Russell, The Story of Leith

When Provost Drummond built the North Bridge in 1796, he contemplated that it should become an access to Leith, as well as to the projected New Town. Indeed, he seems to have been obliged to make it pass altogether under that semblance, in order to conciliate the people: for upon the plate sunk under the foundations of the bridge, it is solely described as the opening of a road to Leith.

Robert Chambers, Traditions of Edinburgh

In the beginning of the present [nineteenth] century, and before the roads to Queensferry and Granton were constructed, the chief or only one in this quarter was that which, between hedgerows and trees, led to Trinity.

James Grant, Old and New Edinburgh

To my Mother
who grew up in Trinity

— TRADITIONS OF — TRINITY AND LEITH

REVISED AND EXTENDED

JOYCE M. WALLACE

Foreword by
DR PETER ROBINSON

JOHN DONALD PUBLISHERS LTD
EDINBURGH

ISBN 0 85976 447 8

British Library Cataloguing in Publication Data
A catalogue record for this book is available from the British Library.

Front cover: Trinity House of Leith.
Back cover: Hay Lodge in East Trinity Road.

Typeset by
Pioneer Associates (Graphic) Ltd, Perthshire
Printed in Great Britain by
Bell & Bain Ltd., Glasgow

Foreword

In a different world Edinburgh might well have been a distant suburb of the City of Leith and not the other way around. For nature had blessed that part of the shore of the Forth will all the advantages of a safe haven and a flat site. It was something that the burgesses of Edinburgh understood well in a more robust age of merchant intrigue. Perched high on a hill two miles from the sea, they had long seen Leith and the shore as a threat to their livelihoods. Their very survival depended on controlling the port and the people, and it was a struggle where power and prestige prevailed.

Almost ninety years of independence from Edinburgh from 1833 to 1920 stamped a mark of individuality on Trinity and Leith that has survived wartime bombs and the more sustained ravages of decay. At one time an Edinburgh-based officialdom might have banished Leithers to Sighthill and beyond, but their hearts remained by the sea. Refugees returned to shop and to reminisce. Happily now more are coming back to work.

The Leith Project, not long under way when the first edition was published in 1985, helped to restore self-confidence to areas blighted by changing trade patterns and more than half a century of neglect. At last there is a future, allowing the natural advantages of location and something of that independent spirit to prevail. In the last dozen or so years houses and shops have sprouted out of empty warehouses, gaps have been filled, and more recently the Scottish Office has moved down to Victoria Quay. A real sense of opportunity is returning.

Leith remains above all a port of rich contrast and unlikely associations, with Trinity its more genteel western suburb.

Together they have looked out to the world. They have weathered tyrants and storms, smugglers, sieges and plague, and there are strong associations with international figures, like Hans Christian Anderson and Robert Louis Stevenson, born in Inverleith. Not that there were any shortages of local characters, such as the cadaverous and asthmatic Hugo Arnot and the notorious Green Jenny who haunted the unwary in the night haar. There was nothing dull about Trinity and Leith past.

This is a story that is unashamedly about the past and it is as much about places as people. Joyce Wallace is an accomplished local historian whose family associations with Trinity and Leith go back more than a century. For many years she has patiently researched and recorded the area from original material and developed an understanding which brings to life Edinburgh's northern shoreline and immediate hinterland. It is a unique and lively record, conveniently gathering material on Trinity in particular.

The new revised and extended edition includes much original information not covered in the first printing or by Joyce Wallace's later *Further Traditions of Trinity and Leith*. Added is the story of Challenger Lodge associated with the early days of marine exploration, and the intriguing history of Trinity Mains Farmhouse, after which Trinity appears to have been named. Secret chambers in Trinity Mains and the neighbouring Woodbine Cottage are explored for the first time, raising questions about a murkier past of smuggling and pressed men. New information has come to light about Granton House, and many other additions and insights are included that help to reinforce *Traditions* as a definitive work.

This is still a book where you can smell the sea salt and watch the trams shuggle in and out of Shrubhill. Joyce Wallace touched the weeping walls of Bangholm Bower and the blood red ochre runs as convincingly as ever.

Edinburgh

Peter Robinson

Introduction

The original text of this book, published in 1985, was based on a series of articles on the subjects of Trinity and Leith and was not therefore written as a continuous, progressive historical account. The opportunity has now been taken to revise, correct, re-arrange and considerably enlarge that text in the light of subsequent research and to rewrite it in a more cohesive and structured format.

In the intervening period a second book, *Further Traditions of Trinity and Leith*, published in 1990, was written from the beginning as a book, and it can be read independently for its own account of this part of Edinburgh or in conjunction with both the first and the present volumes as it contains information not repeated in the others. It also contains suggestions for further reading.

Trinity, so closely linked to Leith from its earliest days and the history of which I have been primarily concerned to write, is still comparatively unspoiled by strident building intrusion into the rich variety of its architectural heritage, but, notwithstanding that it is a designated conservation area, vigilance is required on an ongoing basis to ensure that this is safeguarded for the future.

Edinburgh   J.M.W.

Acknowledgements

Grateful acknowledgement is made to Dr. W. S. Robertson and Dr. P. Barron, whose knowledge of Trinity has been of great assistance in the writing of this book, to the Royal Incorporation of Architects in Scotland who arranged for the reading of the original text by Dr. Peter Robinson, a former President of the Edinburgh Architectural Association, and to the staff of the Edinburgh Room at the Edinburgh Public Library. I am also indebted to Mrs Ann Hope for permission to quote from *Tales of a Great Grand-Aunt* and for information on the life of Miss Frances Hope, and to Captain A. S. Hamilton, Master, Trinity House of Leith, for the Jacobus Prymrose information. My particular thanks go to the artist, Miss Perpetua Pope, the last person to live in Hay Lodge, for allowing me to have copies made of the only photographs now in existence of that fascinating house and for her patience in explaining the lay-out of its interior, and to Mr and Mrs W. Steedman, the owners of Woodbine Cottage, for invaluable help and information and for allowing me to see the place of concealment within the house.

Contents

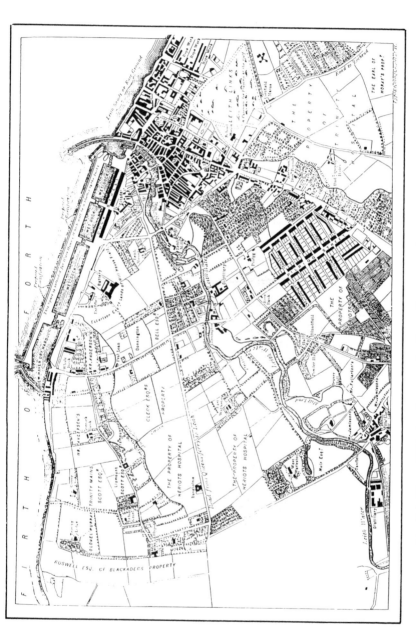

Ainslie's Plan of Trinity showing the Boswall, Scott and Anderson properties.

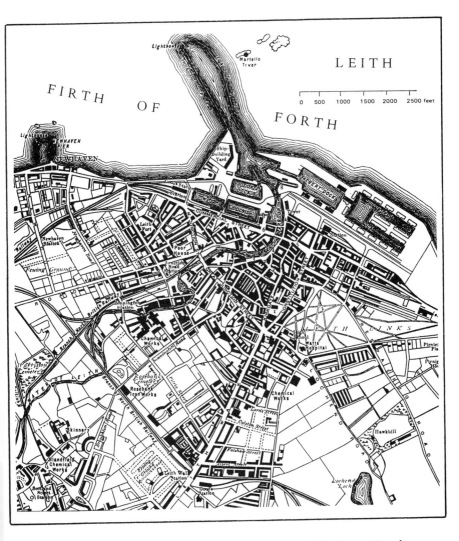

Plan of Leith in 1883. The New Cut to the west of Newhaven Road,
the present-day Craighall Road, was made for the intended use of
George IV after landing at the Chain Pier in 1822. In the event he
came ashore not at Trinity but at Leith.

Except where otherwise stated, illustrations are from photographs by the author.

CHAPTER ONE

Inverleith

Before the New Town of Edinburgh was conceived in progressive civic minds within the cabined, cribbed Old Town in the late 18th century, the City, perched high and narrow on its long volcanic ridge, was flanked on the immediate north by the valley of the Nor' Loch and on the immediate south by the valley of the little River Tumble which had been domesticated into the lower residential thoroughfare parallel to the High Street known as the Cowgate. The wider environment of this rockbound, urban island consisted of rough, open country with scattered farms and hamlets, surrounded on all sides by bogland or muirland and also by lochs and hills. Marshes, dangerous after nightfall to the unwary traveller, lay to the west, stretching out towards Corstorphine village where a lamp was hung in the gable of the Parish Church as a guide to wayfarers before the ground was drained and laid out with roads. To the south lay the Borough Loch, later to be replaced by the green, tree-planted hollow known as The Meadows, and the Borough Muir on which the ancient oaks, that had supplied the timber, or 'timmer', frontages of the High Street houses since the time of James IV, were destined to come down and the residential streets of Marchmont and The Grange (the old Grange of St. Giles having been situated on the moor) to go up during the course of the 19th century. To the east was the sea with its seaport and then, further round the coast, the Figgate Muir, later to be subdued into the popular Victorian bathing resort of Portobello. And on the north, windswept and salt-sprayed from the Firth of Forth, the lands of Wardie spread out their tough and uncompromising old Muir at the foot of the long, exposed hillside that bottomed out in the valley of the Forth, with the Kingdom of Fife across the water.

At a remote period Inverleith was the name given to a very wide stretch of terrain round the mouth of the Water of Leith, then a substantial river, and, as John Russell has pointed out in *The Story of Leith*, the shortened form of Leith was soon adopted by the thriving town which grew from the tiny village then occupying the site now known as The Shore, an area which, as the discovery of skulls, stone hammers and bronze axes testifies, probably witnessed human settlement at an earlier date than Edinburgh. Inverleith – the longer form – was then confined to the lands lying further up the river, and this usage has remained to the present day.

James Grant, the late-19th century historian of Edinburgh, describes the appearance of Wardie Muir, first in its original virgin state and then after its suburban transformation which took place largely in the early decades of last century: 'Wardie Muir must once have been a wide, open and desolate space extending from Inverleith and Warriston to the shore of the Firth; and from North Inverleith Mains, of old called Blaw Wearie, on the west, to Bonnington on the east. . . . Now it is intersected by streets and roads studded with fine villas rich in gardens and teeming with fertility.' But Inverleith itself was sometimes called Innerleith (Inner-lyth on Blaeu's atlas of 1654), and the probability that the Water from which it takes its name was a much larger river in the past than it is now is borne out by a history of periodic flooding in the earlier centuries. The deliberate redirection for industrial purposes of springs feeding the river is probably the main cause of its diminution. The prefix 'Inver' (an alternative form of 'Aber') from the Gaelic 'Inbhir' means a place where sea and river meet, and thus indicates the possibility that the Leith was navigable as far inland as Inverleith or even, as has been claimed, Stockbridge. It was in fact at one time known as 'the Great River of the Water of Leith'. In 1659 there were 'unheard of tempests, storms and inundations of water whilk destroyed ... eleven mills ... upon the Water of Leith'. In 1794 there was a dangerous 'spate in the river', and in 1821 'a coachman with his horse was carried down the stream and drowned near the gate of Inverleith.'

The baronial estate of Inverleith is of ancient origin, having been mentioned in the Charters of Robert the Bruce. In the 15th century it came into the possession of the Touris – or Towers – family who had a town house in Towris, or Towrs, Close (later Mary King's Close) in the High Street of Edinburgh. They were large landowners in the area and among

Inverleith House in the Royal Botanic Garden, an 18th century building which was once the home of the Rocheids of Inverleith.

the missing charters of Robert III are two to William Touris of the lands of Berntoun and of the superiority of King's Cramond. Two hundred years after the Touris ownership Inverleith passed to the strangely named Rocheids, an appellation said to have originated in a physical peculiarity of a member of that family. Sir James Rocheid, who acquired the lands in 1678, had been suspected, while Town Clerk of Edinburgh, of embezzlement but appears successfully to have survived both this and several other stigmas. Another James, the last representative of that line, lived in Inverleith House, built by him in the heart of what is now the Royal Botanic Garden in 1773, and into which he and his mother, Mrs Rocheid of Inverleith, moved when it had become necessary to abandon the earlier and deteriorated house on an adjoining site. Even for those days when extreme formality was more honoured in the acceptance than the breach, they stood on ceremony to such an extent that Lord Cockburn thought it worth recording in his *Memorials*. Grant called him 'a man of inordinate vanity and family pride', and Cockburn, with relish and perhaps a hint of nostalgia, recalled the ostentatious style in which his mother drove out in her mulberry-coloured coach, where she sat 'like a Nautilus in its shell', down the drive which more public-spirited times have pedestrianised into Arboretum Avenue, past the lodge and the gate-piers surmounted by their ancient and curious stone lions said to have come originally from Edinburgh Castle, over the Stock Bridge and so to town, stared after by a local populace suitably awed by her magnificence. On entering an assembly 'she would sail like a ship from Tarshish, gorgeous in velvet or rustling silk' and 'take possession of the centre of a large sofa', covering it 'with her bravery, the graceful folds seeming to lay themselves over it like summer waves.' She presided in similar pomp over her son's dinners 'to the very last day almost of a prolonged life'. The lodge, gate-piers and the lions still identify the old entrance, though their association with Inverleith House now tends to be forgotten.

In 1863 the house and its immediate policies became the domain of the Scottish historian and antiquary Cosmo Innes who claimed he could trace the lands of Inverleith back to their possession by the baker of King William the Lion. Fourteen acres of the Rocheid estate had in 1820 become the permanent location of the Botanic Garden which had first been planted as long ago as 1670 at Holyrood where it was known as the Physic Garden and then transferred in 1763 to another site at Haddington Place in Leith Walk. After the death of Cosmo Innes in 1874 Inverleith House and the surrounding land were bought by the City and added, as an extension, to the Garden where the house provided a finely situated residence for the Keeper. Its adaptation as the National Gallery of Modern Art was carried out in 1960 but the Gallery was resited in 1984 in the former John Watson's School at Belford.

In St. Bernard's Row, leading to the lodge and gate-piers of Inverleith House, the house formerly known as Malta Green has been restored. Built about 1840, such external features as a label moulding on the main frontage and miniature battlements on the roof have lent credance to the description of its architectural style as English Tudor.

The Georgian houses in Inverleith Row, described by Grant as 'handsome villas and other good residences', were planned by Thomas Brown and, starting in 1823, were built on ground which had belonged to the 'eminent agriculturist', James Rocheid. The only survising references to his name within the bounds of his inheritance are the little Rocheid Path which runs by the Water of Leith between the north end of Arboretum Avenue and Canonmills and the much more recent houses at Rocheid Park south of Ferry Road and west of East Fettes Avenue. The ancient village of Canonmills lay within the Barony of Broughton and owed its origin 'to the same source as the Burgh of Canongate, having been founded by the Augustinian Canons of Holyrood'. Here David I built a corn mill for the canons, and also for the use of the local inhabitants, on the south side of the Water of Leith, which was driven by a lade diverted from it at the Dean Village and known as the Great Lade. To this mill the Incorporation of Baxters (Bakers) in the Canongate were 'thirled', being bound either to grind their corn there or to pay a fine. A restored mill building dating from no earlier than the late 17th or early 18th century survives in Canon Street at its junction with Eyre Place. The mills once occupied the whole site down to the cross-roads south-east of Canonmills Bridge.

A most interesting discovery was made when Canonmills Service Station was being rebuilt at the end of 1994 and the beginning of 1995. At the western side of the area, now covered by the Esso shop and immediately eastwards of the east side of Canon Street, a section of the stone-lined mill lade was exposed for a very short time, but just long enough for photographs to be taken by Dr Athol L. Murray, who at once realised its significance when happening to pass the site. This section was the 'tail-lade', into which the water ran after it had turned the wheel, and it had been covered in, probably in the late 19th century, with brick vaulting. The tail-lade ran down Canon Street from the mill building where the lean-to roof indicates the site of the long-departed wheel, and its bypass outlet was clearly visible on the west side. A lintel with the words *The Baxters' Land 1686*, which had been built into one of the previous service station buildings, and an explanatory plaque were later placed on the north-facing wall of the new shop. It is hoped that archaeological investigations will be carried out near Canonmills Bridge where part of the Great, or Main, Lade, which left the Water of Leith at the Dean Village, is also located. After turning mill-wheels in the Dean Village, Stockbridge, Silvermills, Canonmills and Logie Green, the water went back into the river near St. Mark's Bridge.

Canonmills Loch with its wildfowl and, at a much later date, Canonmills House lay further to the south, the house being superseded by Eyre Place Church in 1881 and then by modern flats after the demolition of the church in 1990.

Haig's Distillery in Glenogle Road (originally Water Lane)

The 'tail-lade' from The Canon Mill, looking south up Canon Street, when it was briefly uncovered during the rebuilding of Canonmills Service Station. The outlet for the by-pass can be seen on the right (*Photograph courtesy Dr Athol L. Murray*).

was a well-known feature of Canonmills towards the end of the 18th century, and it was there that one of the 'meal mob' riots took place in 1783. A report was circulating that potatoes and oats were being used for distilling purposes while, in that year of food scarcity and high prices, the people were being left to starve. The Riot Act was read, firearms were issued for defence to the Haig employees and the buildings were saved from destruction, though one of the rioters was killed. The disturbances lasted for several days and plans were made to mobilise the servants of country houses in the vicinity of Edinburgh, if required, to put down the disorders.

The original Canonmills Bridge, consisting of a single arch, was built in 1767 and was of considerable importance as it provided convenient access to Inverleith and Trinity for wheeled traffic, and horse-drawn carriages were soon crossing it on their way to the new country houses that were now being built, small and unpretentious for the most part and intended only for summer occupation. It was replaced in 1840 by a bridge carried over the river (which can still run high and brown with floodwater from its source above Harperrigg Reservoir, into and then out of which manmade sheet of water it flows, after winter snows) on three arches. This later bridge was widened in 1896. To the east, at Warriston Road, the former goods railway line is carried over the street and the stream by a substantial stone viaduct constructed in 1841.

Between the two bridges an 18th-century, whitewashed, pantile-roofed farm cottage has somehow managed to survive in Warriston Road. As it is a farm cottage as opposed to a farm house, it may be supposed that the farm was very small as well with, possibly, a cow or two, perhaps some goats and a few pigs, and it was not difficult to imagine hens strutting and scratching in the little garden which lay in front of the entrance on the other side, away from the road and the river. In the following century it became the gatehouse of Heriot-hill Station and after that the home of a 'mussel boiler' who left it littered with mussel shells. After rescue from dereliction it had the good fortune to be transformed into the Canonmills Pottery and a kiln chimney was attached to its further gable. The pottery, an ideal use for the little building, was subsequently closed as the whole site, which is bounded on the south by Broughton Road, was acquired for building development in 1982, and the garden, which had been restored and replanted as a typical old cottage garden by the potter, was destroyed. Warriston Farm Cottage, however, being the

An 18th century farm cottage that has survived modern housebuilding in Warriston Road.

subject of a preservation order, was given a new lease of life as a photographic processing laboratory with a short extension added on the western side. By 1995 the cottage was empty again and it is now occupied by a firm of architects.

Also at Canonmills, on the north bank of the Water of Leith, was until recently all that remained of what Grant called 'the peculiar edifice known as Tanfield Hall'. It was 'an extensive suite of buildings designed, it has been said, to represent a Moorish fortress, and was erected in 1825 as oil-gas works, but speedily turned to other purposes.' It is principally remembered today as the place in which the first General

Assembly of the Free Church of Scotland was held in 1843 when the Disruption brought well over four hundred protesters against the injustices of patronage out of St. Andrew's Church (now St. Andrew's and St. George's) in George Street and onto 'the long steep street' that led towards Tanfield Hall where they proceeded to elect Dr Thomas Chalmers as their first Moderator. The name is taken from a former Tannery at this point on the riverbank and buildings here were for many years the printing works of Morrison & Gibb. The whole site was cleared of all remaining buildings, including the last remnant of Tanfield Hall, by The Standard Life Assurance Company whose new office buildings, known as Tanfield House, were opened by the Queen in 1991.

No. 8 Inverleith Row, a large classical villa beside the eastern entrance to the Royal Botanic Garden, was designed in 1824 by W. H. Playfair, the architect of the Royal Scottish Academy in Princess Street, who, in 1818, was optimistically appointed architect for a projected New Town between Edinburgh and Leith. The imposing terraces around the Calton Hill and the elegantly classical Windsor Street were built, as well as Hillside Crescent and Leopold Place, but the scheme to extend Edinburgh's Georgian development from Calton to Leith Links was much too grandiose and costly ever to be a practical proposition.

In recent times, Sir Thomas Innes of Learney, the late Lord Lyon King-of-Arms, lived for many years in Inverleith Row at No. 35, as did the Edinburgh historian and writer, the late Moray McLaren, and his actress wife Lennox Milne, at No. 29. The well-known Edinburgh Jewellers, Messrs. Hamilton and Inches, lived here also, the Hamiltons at No. 17 (now an Abbeyfield House) and the Inches at No. 18. Although the last years of his life were spent in Trinity, Horatio MacCulloch, who has been described as 'the artist *par excellence* of Scottish landscape', lived at 54 Inverleith Row in the mid-19th century.

At No. 8 Howard Place, a row of front-gardened terraced

villas built in 1809 on the opposite side of the street and closer to Canonmills, was born, in 1850, the only child of his parents, the delicate boy who was to become known to the world by the three initials, R. L. S. In 1853 the Stevenson family removed to No. 1 Inverleith Terrace, just across the road and previously occupied by William Edmondstoune Aytoun, Professor of Rhetoric at Edinburgh University and famous contributor to *Blackwood's Magazine*, and his wife Jane, daughter of Professor John Wilson, better known to readers of that illustrious publication as Christopher North. (Since 1871 this house, due to later additional building, has been numbered 9.) Both houses proved to be in too damp a locality for the health of Robert Louis and his mother, from whom he had inherited the weak condition of his chest, and in 1857 they left low-lying Inverleith for the windier but drier Heriot Row in the New Town up the hill.

Stevenson's birthplace at 8 Howard Place contained for many years a memorial museum which was open to the public, but the relics and artefacts were removed when the house once more became a private home. They were taken to Lady Stair's House in the Lawnmarket where they are now exhibited along with those of Burns and Scott in The Writers' Museum.

The poet W. E. Henley knew Stevenson well and collaborated with him in an unsuccessful attempt to write a play on the life and crimes of the prototypical Jekyll and Hyde, Deacon William Brodie, later, as all the world knows, to become the subject of a novel written by Stevenson himself. The Henleys lived 'a few doors from R. L. S.'s birthplace', as Eve Blantyre Simpson, daughter of Sir James Young Simpson, wrote in her book *The R. L. Stevenson Originals*. Their only child, 'a beautiful daughter', was born there but died shortly afterwards in London, her 'brief years' having been spent in Edinburgh in Howard Place. Their house was No. 11 and it was during their stay there that Henley edited the *Scots Observer*. Here they were visited by the playwright J. M. Barrie who took a particular interest in their little daughter, Margaret, who used to call him 'Friendy-Wendy', a name Barrie was later to immortalise in *Peter Pan*.

At the foot of the hill leading down from Broughton Road to Canonmills a bronze plaque on the wall of a building at the corner of Munro Place records the fact that it was in a hall here that, about 1857, Stevenson first went to school. Above the inscription is a head of the poet in relief. The building itself, which has been considerably altered since it contained the school, is now Canonmills Baptist Church. At the top of the hill the Royal Navy and Royal Marine Club occupies the 18th century Heriot Hill House on the corner of Broughton Road.

At the north end of Inverleith Row, at Goldenacre, No. 52 was for years the home of a remarkable old army officer, Lieut.-General William Crockat, whose name, says James Grant, 'was associated with the exile and death of Napoleon in St. Helena'. In 1807 he was 'gazetted an ensign in the 20th Regiment of Foot' and saw distinguished service in Spain in the famous battles of Vimiera, Corunna and Vittoria. At the end of the French wars he went with his regiment to the now legendary island of captivity where he became the last officer to be given charge of the 'caged eagle of St. Helena' who died there under his guardianship. The then Captain Crockat was sent home with dispatches to announce the news. After these historic events he spent the rest of his active life in India, retiring in 1830 to Edinburgh where, 'in spite of war, wounds and fever', he lived for nearly half a century before he passed away, in 1874, at a green old age, in his villa at Inverleith Row, 'a hale old relic of other times.'

Close at hand, near the junction with Inverleith Gardens, stands St. James' Episcopal Church, built in the middle Gothic style in 1888 by Sir Rowand Anderson. This spacious church has a beautiful and interesting interior, the chancel walls being painted in fresco with representations of saints and martyrs by William Hole, R.S.A., who was a member of the congregation. Noteworthy also are the figure of the Good Shepherd by C. d'O. Pilkington Jackson and stained glass windows by Douglas Strachan. The congregation united with that of Christ Church, Trinity, in 1980 and with its own former mission church in Canonmills, St. Philip's in Logie Green Road, six years later.

The Presbyterian Inverleith Church, at the top of Granton Road, was built in 1881 by the Free Church of Scotland at a cost of £5000 to replace an earlier iron church erected in 1874 on a different site to meet the needs of people resident in the then comparatively small number of houses in Granton and Wardie. The new building was called the St. James Free

Inverleith Church at the top of Granton Road was built in 1881.

Church, but this was changed to United Free on the union of the Free and United Presbyterian Churches in 1900. The final change came twenty-nine years later when, as Inverleith Parish Church, it assumed its present status as a congregation of the Church of Scotland, the U.F. churches having then returned to the established fold. During the Depression of the 1930s Sunday services for the unemployed were held in the Alhambra Theatre in Leith Walk and a Leith Unemployed Men's Club was started in 1932 with Dr Arthur Cowan, Minister of Inverleith Parish Church, as President.

To the east of Inverleith Row lie the ancient lands of Warriston, and the name 'Warriston House' could until fairly recently, when it was removed on commencement of new housebuilding activity in the grounds of the old mansionhouse itself, be seen on a solitary derelict gate-pier standing, like a stout old tree defying the woodman's axe, at the entrance to the Georgian villa (that replaced an earlier house on the same site) which was demolished, along with the lodge, in the late 1960s. As James Grant remarked, 'Like the house of Inverleith, it must have formed a conspicuous object from the once open . . . expanse of Wardie Muir'. The gates of Warriston (or more correctly West Warriston) House, particularly excellent examples of wrought-iron work, were preserved from destruction during the Second World War by the family of John Best who were the last occupants of the house and who had the foresight to take them down before they fell victim, like all other garden railings, to compulsory annexation for military purposes. Some years later they were set up a few feet inside the west entrance to Drummond Place Gardens where they can still be seen.

A dwellinghouse clearly much older than its neighbours in Inverleith Row, and standing immediately behind an outer wall a short distance northwards from the erstwhile gate-pier, was at one time within the bounds of Warriston House estate and may well have been a gardener's cottage as it adjoins the remains of a curved wall which was probably part of the walled garden of Warriston House. Considerably altered and enlarged in later years, Warriston Cottage (No. 101) dates back to the late 18th century, possibly to around the 1780s.

The Warriston estate was in the possession of the Somervilles in the early 16th century. They were the builders of the original house where, by the 1580s, they had been succeeded by the Kincaids and in which a dark tragedy took place in 1600. Jean Livingston, the wife of John Kincaid of Warriston, who appears to have been badly treated by her husband, persuaded a servant of her father called Robert Weir to do away with him. Both were tried for the murder and sentenced to death. Charles Kirkpatrick Sharpe, who wrote a history of this *cause célèbre*, says that the Lady of Warriston, only twenty-one years of age, accepted her fate with resignation and in a spirit of great contrition . She was executed by the 'Maiden' at the Girth Cross of Edinburgh, reading an address to the assembled spectators, who were moved to compassion by her serenity and courage, from the scaffold. To this account of these events, however, it should be added that recent research by Mrs Z. M. Ashford, who was born in East Warriston House, indicates that they took place in the latter house rather than in that of West Warriston, thus refuting existing historical records.

A later owner is said to have been Sir Archibald Johnston of Warriston but here too the records may have become confused as he took his title from another district called Warriston near Currie and it is therefore likely that he did not in fact live in West Warriston House. A Lord of Session in 1641, he was granted a peerage by Oliver Cromwell. But the honour cost him his life as he was executed in Edinburgh after the Restoration by Charles II.

Warriston Crescent, its elegant houses and rear gardens turning their backs on the Water of Leith at 'Puddocky', was built on the West Warriston estate in the 1820s, and it was here, at No. 10, that Fryderyk Chopin, the Polish composer and musician, stayed in 1848, the year before his death from tuberculosis, when he visited Edinburgh during his last concert tour. A century afterwards a plaque was placed on the wall by the Polish community and their Scottish friends in the city to commemorate the anniversary. Born near Warsaw in 1810, the world-famous pianist was buried in Paris in 1849.

A feature of this area which may have caught Chopin's eye was the toll-house which once stood at the south-west corner of Canonmills Bridge. Further north, Eildon Street was also built on ground feued from the Warriston estate. An Edwardian terrace of tall, narrow villas, it was placed on the perimeter of what is now Lothian Regional Council's Warriston Private Playing Fields, similarly feued, with the deliberate intention of capitalising on the open view back to the skyline of the old city above the First New Town. The site of an ornamental pond is now occupied by tennis courts and this ground becomes very readily waterlogged after heavy rain. Warriston Cemetery, opened in 1843 as the New Edinburgh Cemetery, lies to the east and eastwards of it is Sir Robert Lorimer's Warriston Crematorium. This was created out of East Warriston House, adapting to a very different purpose the villa built in 1808 for Andrew Bonar of Ramsay Bonar & Co., one of the banks whose loans enabled the Georgian development of the New Town to be financed. Mrs Ashford's most interesting and informative paper on *The Lands of Warriston* in the *Book of the Old Edinburgh Club* (New Series Vol. 3 1994) includes a photograph of the house prior to its conversion.

On the north side of Ferry Road, northwards and westwards of Inverleith Row, the playing fields, known as Ferryfield, of the former Melville College for boys were laid out over the fertile soil of Windlestrawlee Farm, quaintly so called after the crested dogtail grass known as windlestrae, a name, says Grant, which was also applied in Scotland to bent and stalks of grass found on moorish ground. A path bordered with white stones led to the farmhouse, a small, whitewashed one-storeyed cottage which was extended as a byre, the difference

Houses have now replaced these old Windlestrawlee farm buildings
on the north side of Ferry Road.

between the two sections being windows and a chimney in
the house and skylights in the byre roof for the animals. The
Ferryfield entrance gates (no longer here) were presented by
former pupils of the school at their Club centenary in 1965.
On the other side of the road the farm of North Inverleith
Mains later became the playing fields of Daniel Stewart's
College, one of the four Edinburgh Merchant Company
schools. When Melville College amalgamated with Stewart's
College, Ferryfield became the property of the Company and
was sold by them in 1981. Now laid out with the new streets
of Wardie Park, Ferryfield and West Ferryfield, a residential
development has spread across the whole playing field area and

the little farmhouse has been swept away. To the immediate west lie the houses of West Winnelstrae.

The city's roots may be deep in its native earth, but Edinburgh is far from being a town planted on the plains: so far indeed as to have had a built-in public transport problem from time immemorial, a difficulty later partially overcome by the building of inumerable bridges. Sparing a thought or two for the ups and downs of life at the present day if these levellers of the terrain were suddenly to vanish brings some realisation of what it was like to go hither and yon before they were built. But there were no such short cuts to be engineered on the steep slope northwards from the New Town to Inverleith and, even with the addition of a trace horse, it often proved to be too stey a brae for the horse trams which carried passengers through the less precipitous streets from the mid-19th century until more sophisticated methods were introduced. The first solution to the problem was found in the 1880s when underground cable traction was installed and operated from a power station and depot in Henderson Row, a building which has since been demolished with the exception of the facade (with the words 'Edinburgh Corporation Tramways' still carved below the roofline) which has been incorporated into a much larger building constructed in 1991 for the Scottish Life Assurance Company. Until 1920 the much-maligned cable cars (which, compared to the 'bus, possessed a picturesque dignity more germane to the ocean-going liners that reached the height of their popularity at the same time) were hauled up the hillside, breaking down more frequently as time went on, their route taking them along Inverleith Row from Goldenacre to Canonmills and up Hanover Street, and then back in the reverse direction.

In the days before urban development had laid its civilising influence across the Wardie Muir, the northern landscape was one of long views over trees and fields and undulating grassland to the sea, with an occasional farm or country house in the middle distance. The Water of Leith flowed on its hard-working way from the upstream mills (there were seventy mills as well as tanneries and other industries along its length) to those at Bonnington and the port. And when the dwellers in the Old Town would fare abroad, they rode on horseback or, having descended by Leith Wynd to the Calton valley and climbed up on the other side, set out on foot to their destination, Leith itself perhaps, or Stockbridge, or the rich Rocheid farmlands of Inverleith.

CHAPTER TWO

Trinity

'Are you another antiquary?', enquired the local resident, domiciled in one of its modern neighbours, as the camera recorded, in a burst of sunshine, the only surviving remnant of the once large and venerable House of Wardie. Bereft of its principal structural components, it hides its crow-stepped, unassuming dignity and its one remaining graceful seaward turret well out of sight behind the trafficways, the former spaciousness of its surroundings now reduced to a tiny fragment of front garden where a few low shrubs and white-helmeted snowdrops were defying the elemental weather on this mad March morning. It was one of those typical 'Edinburgh' days when cold March winds and biting April showers, alternating with a sudden piercing sun, produced Stevenson's 'downright meteorological purgatory' for one half-hour, and June suns and blue skies of Mediterranean brilliance for the next. 'That's the west wing' (though it is in fact the kitchen premises, left standing when the rest was demolished), went on the local resident, clutching his hat, 'all that's left of the old place. The main, central part was here, where we're standing; it's been gone for donkeys' years. And it took a pitched battle with officialdom to save this final bit from a similar fate in the 1960s.'

It was near the old castle of Wardie that, in 1544, the Earl of Hertford landed with an army of ten thousand soldiers. This invading host had been sent by Henry VIII 'to burn Edinburgh . . ., to sack Leith', and to put 'man, woman and child to fire and sword', in an attempt to take Mary, the infant Queen of Scots, by force when the treaty with England under which she was betrothed to Edward, Henry's son, went

The surviving remnant of the once large and ancient house of
Wardie, still used as a private dwellinghouse.

unfulfilled. Hertford was soundly beaten, but a high price was
paid in life and property to disengage the Queen, too young
to be troubled by the first tumult of her tempestuous life,
from this 'rough wooing'. The old fortalice of Wardie is mentioned again in a charter of 1605 when it appears to have been
in the possession of Sir John Tours, or Touris, of Inverleith
who has been already mentioned in Chapter 1. About fifty
years later stones from 'the ruinous manor of Wardie' were
being used, along with others from nearby villages, to build
Cromwell's Citadel in Leith. It must have been rebuilt, however, as a mansionhouse is known to have been here in 1780,
the property of Sir Alexander Boswall of Wardie House

whose name is perpetuated in Boswall Road and who will re-enter the Trinity story in Chapter 4.

The short side street opens up at this end into a square bounded by the low walls of another and sharply contrasting house with stiff, Grecian symmetry and columned portico, on the other side, standing in greensward as neat and spreading as Wardie's cottage garden is confined and wild. (This view is now obscured by additional buildings at St. Columba's Hospice.) 'Challenger Lodge', said my informant, waving his hand in the direction of the wall. 'There's an interesting story connected with it. It belonged to a seafaring man in the 19th century – quite a character they say. He was asked to sail

Challenger Lodge where navigation charts were drawn up in the 1870s is now St. Columba's Hospice.

round the world, no less, and then to draw up navigation charts from the scientific information obtained during protracted soundings in the seven seas. He came back here afterwards and wrote it all up, calling the house, formerly Wardie Lodge, after his ship *The Challenger*. They're still in use today, those charts, so he must have been the right man for the job.' This intrepid mariner was Sir John Murray, K.C.B., F.R.S. (1841–1914), an oceanographer with the *Challenger* Expedition of 1872–76, and after that voyage of discovery he edited the reports, which ran to fifty enormous volumes, in this pleasant villa which had been built in 1825. The history of the house, now a hospice, and its interesting successive occupants is given in the next chapter.

Westward of this historic enclave, the unsheltered walls of the former Royal Forth Yacht Club (on the site of the original entrance to Wardie House) have withstood many an equinoctial gale stirred up by the spirits of the Firth who had been early at their boisterous work that morning. A huge anchor had found a peaceful mooring out of the waves' way by the wall in front of the forecourt of the Club, and I leaned over to read the inscription, momentarily bright or darkened by the scudding clouds, as it became decipherable. It had been 'lost during the siege of Leith in 1564 when Queen Elizabeth sent her fleet under Admiral Winter who bombarded Inchkeith which was successfully held by the Scotch and French troops under General D'Essé.' The anchor was recovered in 1899 by Mr D. Armit and presented by his widow to the club. It might well have been on such a day as this that an armed fleet, on the orders of the redoubtable Protestant Queen, entered the waters of the Firth of Forth or, as it is called on Blaeu's Atlas of 1654, 'Edenburgh Fyrth', for an abortive trial of strength with the island's defenders, and it is not hard to imagine one of them being blown off course and foundering on some rocky coastal defile. Or perhaps, in an attempt to hold the ship at anchor after nightfall, the massive iron hook was fouled by some submerged obstruction from which the vessel had to be cut free at dawn as the ships withdrew from the encounter and made the best of their way back to the open sea. The Royal Forth Yacht Club building has been converted into flats and the club itself, taking the old anchor with it, has removed to Granton.

Round the corner, entered by the vertical iron rails through which no creels could pass and long known as the Fishwives' Puzzle, Wardie Steps descend to Granton and sea level at the western extremity of Trinity. Before it was chosen as a dormitory suburb in which to build their streets of gardened villas by the merchants of the Port, it was part of the

An old anchor from the Siege of Leith when it was outside the former Royal Forth Yacht Club in Boswall Road. Both are now re-sited at Granton.

24

desolate and extensive Wardie Muir, that undulating wasteland, already mentioned, between Inverleith and the sea, bounded on the east by Bonnington and crossed by the Anchorfield Burn. And much earlier than that, in prehistoric times, glaciers covered the whole area and the sea was far to the east of the Forth Valley. This was during the period of the last Ice Age about ten to fifteen thousand years ago, when the whole country was depressed by the weight of a great sheet of ice as much as two thousand feet deep. When the ice melted and flowed slowly away from west to east, the ground began to rise again to a considerable height above sea level, and it was the resultant raised beach that became the Wardie Muir on which Trinity, with its sudden steep drops down the cliff face to the shore-line at the foot, was later to be built.

Here, after David I had founded Holyrood Abbey in 1128, its Augustinian monks set up their farms (with their mills further up the hill at Canonmills) and the land did not pass out of their possession till the reign of James IV who bought 143 acres of the Muir from the Abbot in 1505 to construct a harbour for shipbuilding at Newhaven. Grant writes of several fragments of human remains being discovered there, along the coast of Wardie, in 1846 when excavations for a bridge for the Granton Railway line were being carried out, which appeared to be evidence of the 'occupation of the soil at a very remote period by native tribes.' Silver and copper coins of Spanish origin were also found, and tales were rife of 'some great galleon' from the Armada which had been 'cast away upon the rocky coast.'

In July 1558, when the marriage of the Queen of Scots to the French Dauphin, this time an unopposed and peaceful if short-lived alliance, was celebrated in her native country, ten shillings Scots was paid to the pioneers who fired the Royal Salute from Mons Meg, that legendary piece of ordnance at Edinburgh Castle, and the 'bullet' (in those days 'shotted guns' were sometimes used on such occasions) was afterwards retrieved two miles away on the Wardie Muir. (The 'bullet', being a heavy cannon-ball, was clearly not thought to be expendable but worth the trouble of recovering for future use.) All that, though, was a long while since, and the rough old muir has been suburbanised and tamed out of recognition.

The lands of Trinity were held successively by the Logans of Bonnington, the Grays of Warriston and then Evan MacGregor (he may have been Welsh on his mother's side as he changed his name to Evan Evans) who held the office of Bailiff for the Crown and to whom reference will be made later. It may be mentioned in passing that J. Campbell Irons, in *Leith and its Antiquities*, apparently believed that the land was owned by MacGregor in his own right as he states that about the beginning of the late 18th century 'the land around Newhaven, or most of it, appears to have belonged to "Evan MacGregor, of Newhaven", who in 1710 entailed all his lands there, the date of tailzie being August 1707.' The Reform Act of 1832 extended the boundaries of Leith which, to quote again from *Leith and its Antiquities*, ran 'from a point a little to the east of Seafield Toll in a straight line to the western side of Lochend, where the feeder joins the Loch; thence in a straight line to Pilrig Free Church; thence along Pilrig Street and Bonnington Road to the point where the latter [via Great Junction Street] joins the Ferry Road; along Ferry Road to a point a few yards west of Granton Road; thence in a straight line to the sea, at a point where the Wardie Burn joins the Firth of Forth.' The whole area of Trinity was therefore included within these boundaries. Under the 1832 Act one member was returned to Parliament by the Leith district of burghs (i.e. Leith, Portobello and Musselburgh).

Opposite the Georgian porticos of Trinity Crescent, feued about 1824 when sea bathing was becoming popular in Trinity and before the sands of Portobello superseded it, the Chain Pier had been built out into the water. It was erected in 1821 by Sir Samuel Brown, R.N., at a cost of £4000 for steam packets plying between the ports on the Firth of Forth as they were prevented, by the shallowness of the water, from using Leith. When King George IV paid his famous visit to Edinburgh the following year, it was considered as a possible disembarkation point, instead of The Shore at Leith, for the sacred foot of Majesty. (As there was a Chain Pier at Brighton (the only other one ever built), with which the king had such strong connections, it would not have been inappropriate.) But Trinity had to forego that honour; the claims of Leith to be the royal port of entry for the Scottish nation were too well founded to be set aside. It did, however, receive the feet of a very different and this time departing monarch, the exiled Charles X of France. Having become bankrupt in his efforts to counter the French Revo-lution, the youngest brother of Louis XVI had twice been welcomed to Holyrood Palace under the rights of sanctuary for debtors possessed by the abbey and the ancient royal park, but in 1832, with old-style, pre-Revolution monarchy anathema in France and the newly passed Reform Act decreasing his popularity in Edinburgh, he and his household stepped from the Chain Pier on to a steam packet bound for Hamburg on the 18th of Sep-tember. He had become an anachronism in his own lifetime and died five years afterwards, aged 79.

Not being suitable for large vessels, the Chain Pier was soon abandoned for the advantages of Granton Harbour. 'Great swimming Competitions' were held frequently between the Pier and Newhaven Harbour on Saturdays and were conspic-uously advertised in the local newspaper. A frail and narrow structure (it was only four feet wide), it fell eventually into disrepair and was finally swept away in a storm in October 1898. The Chain Pier Inn now occupies the little building which was once the booking office for the steamers and was subsequently extended. Until recently it contained photo-graphs of the pier, and its shattered remains after the storm, but they are no longer on display.

In the third quarter of the 18th century, when the New Town of Edinburgh was abuilding, the 'sylvan suburb' of Trinity was a pleasant stretch of countryside on the shores of Forth with all the makings of a fine, healthful holiday resort. It was not unnatural therefore that those who could afford to leave their tumbling tenements and needier neighbours in the old, overcrowded city for a new town house of space and grace in the very new New Town should see in Trinity the ideal situation for their country villas. Nor had its qualities gone unobserved by the no less affluent merchants and shipowners of the Port. For them, it was an obvious and even more convenient place of potential residence. So the ground which the Fraternity of Masters and Mariners of Trinity House (which building, together with South Leith Church, are all that now remains of the ancient Kirkgate) had bought in 1713 from the aforementioned Evan MacGregor, the Queen's Bailiff (Queen Anne's reign did not end till the following year) by whom the land was administered for the Crown, became the site of active, and in some cases during the Victorian period one might be forgiven for suspecting pretentious, private building operations.

The Trinity House officials had been responsible for laying out the farm of Trinity Mains which had in time given its name to the whole area. Dr James Scott Marshall explains the adoption of the word 'Trinity' as a place name. Throughout the Middle Ages in England and Scotland it was customary for the charitable foundations of mariners to be dedicated to the Holy Trinity, and Trinity Houses are therefore to be found in most seaports. Leith, however, would seem to have been an exception to this rule. No records have been discovered of a chapel or an alter so dedicated within St. Mary's (now South Leith) Church, but the dedication of the church itself to St. Mary is significant as she was the patron saint of mariners. The Masters and Mariners' 'hospital' in the Kirkgate, built in 1555 (rebuilt 1816) was called Fraternity House and this in time became corrupted to, or, to quote Dr Marshall, known 'colloquially' as, Ternity House and then Trinity House. This name was given to their farm of Trinity Mains and the district that grew up around the farm acquired the same name by 'use and wont'. The later history of the farmhouse, after it had passed out of the possession of the Masters and Mariners, is given in Chapter 4.

A map, dated 1838, of Trinity Mains Farm is in Trinity House, and also a Transcription, by the Leith historian John Russell, F.S.A. Scot., of a document which would appear to indicate that Trinity House was of sufficient importance in the early 17th century to justify its affairs being brought to the notice of the king. In 1636 a letter from Charles I was sent to the Bishop of St. Andrews requesting him to investigate some financial irregularities at the 'Hospital', as it was known because of its charitable status. The Bishop was Jacobus Prymrose (of the same family as the future earls of Rosebery) who was Clerk to the Privy Council from 1602 to 1641 and who was also the father-in-law of George Heriot, jeweller and banker to James VI. The document is the minute recording the Bishop's compliance with Charles I's request and it shows that he took the same action to deal with the matter as would in all probability be taken today in such circumstances – he set up a committee!

At Edinburgh, 13th December, 1636.
Forsameikle as the King's Majestie being informed that there hes beene some abuses and disorders in the managing of these things belonging to the hospitall of Leith which apperteaneth to the mariners, & that the Lords of his Majestie's Privie Counsell have taken great care to sie what hath beene disordered there reduced againe to the right use, his Majestie for this effect out of his princelie & pious care of the weele of the said hospitall, hes recommended to the saids Lords to give order how the yeerlie accompts of the said hospitall sall be made that it may appeare that all things are orderlie & piouslie done & quhairas the necessitie of others his Majestie's weightie affaires will not permit the haill Counsell to attend this business thairfore the saids Lords hes nominat & appointed & be the tenor heirof nominats and appoints John, Earle of Traquaire, Lord Heich Thesaurer of this Kingdome, Thomas Lord Binning, William Lord Alexander,

David Bishop of Edinburgh, Sir John Hay, Clerk of Register, Sir John Hamilton of Orbeston, Justice Clerk, or anie thrie of thame, the Lord Thesaurer being one, to conveene & meit when & quhair they sall appoynt & to informe thameselves (after heiring of the Mariners) anent the treid estat of the hospitall & to prescryve some good reules & orders how yeerlie accompts sall be made of the rent of the said hospitall & to consider the decreits concerning the hospitall & to cleere the differences if anie be thairin, & to sie the moneyes decerned putt to ane profitable use for the weele of the hospitall & otheris conforme to the decreits gevin thairanent, as lykwayes to heere the toune of Edinburgh & reasons to be proponed be thame for cleiring thair interessts to the auditors of the saids compts to the intent they may give their approbatiouns & allowance thairunto.

Extracted from the books of the Acts of the Privy Council by me, Jacobus Prymrose, Clerk of same under my sign and subscription manual.

'JACOBUS PRYMROSE'

In the mid-19th century part of the old farmhouse of the Mariners on the north side of East Trinity Road was said to have been incorporated in the larger and now demolished Hay Lodge which was replaced by flats in the 1960s. This later house, somewhat obscured from sight by trees and enclosed by a wall, had the reputation of having been occupied by a sea captain who built a tower in the garden in front of, but not attached to, the house to provide himself with a view of the Firth of Forth. The tower, a tall, narrow structure with a pyrammidal roof, was certainly there but the Post Office Directories make no mention of a sea captain as having lived in the house. In the garden, also, was an ancient vinery with eighteen vines.

After its ownership by the enterprising Alexander Scott (described in Chapter 4) Trinity Mains Farmhouse had a succession of occupants beginning with the local builder George Gunn (who built Mary Cottage) and his son, George Gunn Jnr., an engineer, during the years 1842–45. During the last two of these years an additional occupant was James Russell, a gardener. James Russell was joined by another gardener, James Mackay, for a number of years, but from 1850 to 1852 the name of James Robertson, an accountant, is also given at Trinity Mains House. In 1853 James Robertson is recorded as living at 'Trinity bank'.

In 1855 James Mackay was still at Trinity Mains but the name of the house now changes to Hay Lodge occupied (and presumably owned) by D. Clunie Gregor, Secretary of the Colonial Life Assurance Company, who moved there from No. 7 George Street, the Colonial Life being at No. 5. By 1856 James Mackay is stated to be living in 'Trinity house cottage' which must have been on the Trinity Mains estate. If D. C. Gregor was responsible for the reconstruction and enlargement of the farmhouse (when it became Hay Lodge), he stayed there for a surprisingly short time. In 1857, while still secretary of the Colonial Life, his house is given as No. 28 Danube Street and he does not appear again at Hay Lodge. By 1857 or '58 the gardeners seem to have finally departed from Trinity Mains.

The next occupant was Lieut.-Colonel Ranken who was at Hay Lodge for only two years and who was followed by Isaac Anderson Henry, S.S.C., described as 'of Woodend', whose office was at No. 1 George Street and who remained at Hay Lodge from 1860 until 1884. 'Miss Gillespie' is recorded from 1885, together, for several years, with A.R. Gillespie of Gillespie & Cathcart, Leith commission agents, until 1911.

In the two Directories for 1912/13 and 1913/14 Hay Lodge is not mentioned. It is at this time, however, that the name 'Dulham' would be expected to appear but, although the change in the name of the house to 'Dulham Towers' is reputed to have been made by a manager of The Standard Life Assurance Company called Dulham, no reference to this name is to be found in these two volumes. Furthermore, no-one of that name was manager of the Standard Life during these years.

The name of the penultimate owner, who is previously

recorded as at No. 27 York Road, Trinity, makes its first appearance in the 1914/15 Directory, but the name of the house is still given as 'Hay Lodge.' It therefore looks as if he renamed the house himself as it is in the 1915/16 Directory that this changes to 'Dulham Towers'. The origin of this name and that of the builder of the tower (and its building date) are therefore two additional enigmas (a third will be referred to later) at Hay Lodge. (The name Hay Lodge is mentioned in *Place Names of Edinburgh and the Lothians* (1912) by John Milne, where it is said to be of Gaelic origin and to mean 'fold' or, if a personal name, to have been originally given to a person coming from a fold.)

The new owner in the year of the outbreak of the First World War was Frederick Richard Graham-Yooll, a man much addicted to sporting activities who kept and raced several greyhounds and engaged in the dubious practice of cock-fighting for which a room in the house was, no doubt illegally, set aside. (Campbell Irons records that 'a cockpit for cockfighting had been established on Leith Links in 1702', admission costing 10d (about 4p), 7d and 4d. Such activities in the streets were forbidden two years later, but in the early 19th century there was a cockpit on Leith sands.) Fred Graham-Yooll, as he was always called, was well known as the owner of the Gaiety Theatre (which he turned into a cinema) in Leith, the Princes Cinema at the west end of Princes Street and the Marine Gardens, then a concert hall and place of popular amusement including Ballroom dancing and indoor roller-skating, in Portobello (which later became a depot for city buses), and it is for the latter that he was probably best known.

The son of Andrew Graham-Yooll, an oilworks proprietor, and born at Uphall, as a young man he joined the firm of W. Graham-Yooll & Company, builders' merchants, and later launched out on his own, his first venture being the acquisition of sand quarries. As proprietor of the Sandhills Company he owned many sand pits in the vicinity of Edinburgh. Later, however, he decided to enter the world of the 'amusement caterer' and sports promoter, his aim, in which he had considerable success, being the provision of what would today be called leisure facilities which he intended should rival those at Blackpool, and he was largely instrumental in the opening of many of Edinburgh's highly popular picture-houses. He had himself been a boxer in his youth and later on took up the sport of shooting.

In 1931 he left Dulham Towers for, as it turned out to be, the last time, his intention being to spend the summer at Slipperfield, West Linton, with a relative, Dr Graham-Yooll (probably his nephew who was the local doctor). But he died there unexpectedly of ptomaine poisoning, aged 65, in June of that year after which a brief account of his life was given in the *Edinburgh and Leith Observer*. A widower during his later years, he was survived by his son and two daughters. William Graham-Yooll, his brother, a cement and oil merchant, was at one time Treasurer of the Burgh of Leith. There is a memorial, in the form of a sundial, to Dr Graham-Yooll in West Linton.

Dulham Towers, a long, rambling house consisting of ground, first and second storeys, with a plethora of roof gablets of differing sizes and bargeboarding and therefore Victorian in appearance, then seems to have remained unoccupied until 1936 when it was bought by its last owner, John R. Pope, by a strange coincidence the general manager of yet another insurance company, this time the Caladonian. He changed the name back to Hay Lodge and, after his and his wife's death, it was sold by his daughter to a building contractor who demolished it in 1967.

The only visible links with its past on the ground today are the Hay Lodge nameplates at the entrance to the modern flats and a blocked-up well in the grass a short distance behind the low wall which no doubt provided the tenant farmer of Trinity Mains with his water supply (and which was possibly fed by the same underground stream as supplied Mary Cottage). But the house had another feature after its conversion to Hay Lodge, although whether it was part of Trinity

A blocked-up well can still be seen from East Trinity Road on the
Trinity Mains Farmhouse/Hay Lodge site.

Mains Farmhouse (and it would be easier to explain it if it
were) cannot now be known with absolute certainty. This was
a small hiding place, or secret compartment, and it and the
purpose for which it may have been used are considered in
Chapter 4 along with another, rather different, place of concealment in Woodbine Cottage in York Road.

The oldest surviving house in Trinity is Trinity Lodge, at the
foot of Stirling Road, built in 1774 by Robert Johnston, an
Edinburgh merchant, but it is now flatted and has a modern
house within its garden, a fate that has befallen a number of
properties in the district. But the more interesting, and the
most secluded, dwelling is the slightly later Trinity Grove in
Trinity Road, built in 1790 by David Hunter of Blackness in
Angus, whose son Alexander was a partner in the publishing
firm of Constable & Co. The house has been described as
'simple late Georgian vernacular' and still stands where it did,
although it is now surrounded by later additions including

Trinity Lodge, in Stirling Road, was built in 1774. Many ships'
masters had invested money in Trinity, and several streets were
called after their vessels, Stirling Road after the paddle-steamer
Stirling Castle, built in 1884 for the Forth coastal trade, and Zetland
Place after *The Earl of Zetland*, which sailed between Leith and
Shetland, Zetland being the name used by the Dundas family when
they became Earls of Zetland (or Shetland). Lennox Row and
Lomond Road are also called after ships.

the statutory tower, erected, it may be, in a last desperate
attempt to obtain the view, so beloved by the early Trinity
villa builders, over the chimney stacks of its proliferating
neighbours. Unlike Trinity Lodge, it no longer has its original
name and, with a beautiful garden, is well enclosed by its
walls; only a glimpse can be caught from outside of intriguing

features such as ornamental stone urns and roof-top storks.

Alexander Hunter was bought out of Constable's company in 1811 and died the following year, the little villa being sold to William Creech as a summer residence. Mr Creech was well known in Edinburgh as bookseller, publisher and Lord Provost. His shop, previously owned by Allan Ramsay, was in Creech's Land in the Luckenbooths beside St. Giles, and Chambers writes of these premises as a 'Lounger's Observatory, for seldom was the doorway free of some group of idlers ... Creech himself, with his black silk breeches and powdered head, being ever a conspicuous member of the corps'. Perhaps because of his advancing years, he made no alterations to the house and concentrated his attention on the garden, growing fruit and vegetables with the assistance of a gardener. When he died unmarried in 1815 Trinity Grove, continuing its literary connections, passed to John Ballantyne, the most interesting and by far the most flamboyant of its owners and brother of the more famous James who was printer and, to their mutual undoing, business collaborator of Sir Walter Scott.

John was by this time an auctioneer with premises in Hanover Street which he later exchanged for Waterloo Place. He himself had a fine collection of *objects d'art* at Trinity Grove, which he rechristened 'Harmony Hall' during his incumbency, but most noteworthy were his 'portraits of beautiful actresses' such as Pegg Woffington and Kitty Clive, as John Gibson Lockhart points out in his *Life of Scott*. The ebullient auctioneer made a practice of entertaining the famous theatrical personalities of the day at Harmony Hall when they had engagements in Edinburgh, and actors as famous as Kean, Braham and Kemble displayed their talents for the enjoyment of John and his guests, among whom Scott and Constable were frequently included. Besides his table furnished with many delicacies, John Ballantyne's stable was no less well provided, and he 'usually rode up to his auction on a tall milk-white hunter, yclept Old Mortality, attended by a leash or two of greyhounds'.

Trinity Grove. The original 1790 house is on the left, with part of the Ballantyne extension, with roof stork, on the right.

Trinity Grove. On the right is the low additional wing which John Ballantyne built for his own exclusive use.

He built a large addition to the house about 1816, more than doubling its size, and it is on the roof of the Ballantyne part (now a separate house) that the storks and urns, best seen from the garden at the back, provide interest and embellishment. To his extended residence he attached a wing for his own personal use, and in order to keep out his wife – 'the handsome and portly lady', as Lockhart describes her, 'who bore his name' – he had the entrances made so narrow that she could not 'force her person through any one of them'. The auctioneer, being small and consumptive, had no such difficulty. He was given to playing on a French horn 'with an energy by no means prudent in the state of his lungs', and as early as 1821, when he was only forty-seven, his name appears for the last time in the Post Office Directories as the owner of Trinity Grove. He retired to lead a quiet, rural life in Roxburghshire, but returned to his brother's house in Edinburgh where he died on 16th June of that year and was buried in the Canongate Churchyard. But the 'villa near to the Firth' had witnessed the colourful, though brief, enactment of a rich slice of Edinburgh history as the home of just such a thriftless but kenspeckle character as only her 'golden age' could have thrown up. Sir Walter Scott and George Hogarth, W.S., the father-in-law of Charles Dickens, were two of John Ballantyne's trustees and sold 'Harmony Hall' later in that same year.

In the latter part of the 19th century Trinity Grove belonged to Richard Mackie, a self-made man equally typical of his time as John Ballantyne had been of his. Born in Dunfermline, at an early age he joined a firm of shipbrokers in Leith and thus embarked on a career which was to lead him straight to financial success and civic honour. In 1873, before he was twenty-five, he had become sole proprietor and, going into partnership with his brother-in-law, steered the business into coal exporting as Mackie, Koth & Co. The firm of Richard Mackie & Co., Shipowners, was founded in 1882. He was three times Provost of Leith, and on his receiving a knighthood in June 1909 the *Leith Observer* devoted considerable space to an account of his life, with photographs of himself and his wife. A bust of Sir Richard had been commissioned 'to adorn the vestibule of Leith Town Hall', and tribute was paid to all he had done 'to sweeten the relationship between the Corporations of Edinburgh and Leith'.

In 1927 the house was subdivided, and the southern part of the garden ground became the building site for a western extension of East Trinity Road. An interesting booklet, *The Story of an Old Edinburgh House*, giving historical details of Trinity Grove, was written by the late R. Leslie Hunter, F.S.A., F.S.A. Scot. Mr Hunter had been an iron founder in Falkirk, taking over the management of Cockburn's Foundry in 1930 and continuing in that position until 1954 when he was appointed manager of the Northern Group of Allied Works. He retired in 1962 and died at his home, the Ballantyne extension of the former Trinity Grove, on 13th July 1990, aged 91.

According to Grant, the landscape painter Horatio MacCulloch, R.S.A., lived latterly in a villa adjoining Trinity Grove and died there on 15th June 1867, the same year as the poet Alexander Smith. Cumberland Hill says that MacCulloch 'died at St. Colme Villa Trinity' and mentions the inscribed Runic cross over his grave in Warriston Cemetery.

South Trinity Road and Trinity Road are the original road through Trinity, and the irregular line of the latter is due to its having been drawn round the edge of the fields, which then lay across the Wardie Muir, as it wound northwards towards the sea. To the west of Trinity Grove, on the opposite side of the street, was Trinity Hut, an example of the small (though they were sometimes quite spacious Georgian houses) summer retreats built on the then city outskirts, usually by the owners of large town residences, another example in the Trinity area being Leith Mount which has been superseded on its site by Leith Town Hall and Public Library at the eastern end of Ferry Road. Yet another called Lilyput (later corrupted to Lilypot or Lilypothall) was where the Telephone Exchange now stands in Clark Road. Houses for permanent, year-round occupation came later, especially after the advent of the railway.

Trinity Hut was the home, in the 18th century, of a French *émigré* called Pierre de la Motte who had decided to set up a school of dancing in Edinburgh. As a master of the Terpsichorean art, he achieved the unlikely notoriety of getting on the wrong side of the law on several occasions. In 1742 John Mitchell of Windlestrawlee made complaints to the Burlaw Court in Leith to the effect that de la Motte was 'overrunning his cornfields' when out hunting, the offending hunting party consisting of eight or nine gentlemen and 'twa dogs'. The outcome of the case does not appear to have been recorded and, indeed, it may never have been heard because the defendant calmly sent a friend to tell the Court he was unable to attend as the hearing coincided with his dancing lessons! Two years later he was again brought before the Burlaw Court, this time accused of filling in a ditch, and in yet another brush with authority he was charged with making off with his neighbour's 'fulzie', or manure, to fertilise his own ground at Trinity Hut.

The 'parcel of land' owned by Lamotte (as his name is also written) was called, presumably for some good but forgotten reason, The Welsh Melon, and in 1759 he also had an acrimonious encounter with his immediate neighbour Walter Neilson, a Canongate merchant and the tenant farmer at Trinity Mains, over the ownership of a ditch which was the disputed boundary between the two properties and which had been ploughed up by Neilson without the Pursuer's (Lamotte's) consent.

The servants of several houses in the vicinity were called as witnesses and thereby provided an insight into the early appearance of the area. William Scott, Herd to Patrick Anderson at Laverochbank, said he had known the grounds of Trinity Mains and The Welsh Melon for forty years, before Trinity House of Leith had enclosed their farm with a wall (in 1715) and before Lilyput and other houses, and the Dyke at

Wardie, had been built. At that time there had been a road running westward from Lamotte's house along the north side of the Dyke which the tenants of Wardie, Windlestrawlee and Trinity Mains had used for the purpose of 'leading dung'. After Wardie Dykes had been built he had become servant to Sir James Rocheid of Inverleith who had put up the Dyke and made steps and a stile. John Dick, groom to the old Stage Coach Office in Leith, had seen a cow belonging to Mr Rennie (a previous Trinity Mains tenant) eating the grass on the bottom of the Ditch.

At the end of the hearing it was found proven that both parties to the dispute were 'in use to cut and pasture the grass in the Ditch'. It was then ordained that the Defender (Neilson) was 'to desist from troubling and molesting the Pursuer (Lamotte) in the possession of the Ditch in all time coming'. Neilson was also 'found liable in the Pursuer's Expenses' which were modified to £3.

Lamotte, an over-enthusiastic if many-sided character, was a keen gardener, and his 'evergreen oaks' are said to have been a feature of this part of Trinity till long after his own time.

One of the houses built on ground feued from Alexander Scott of Trinity Mains is Mary Cottage, as it was called at first and to which name it has recently reverted after being known as St. Marie's, in East Trinity Road, which was built in 1823 and has a doorway, behind its front garden, flanked by Ionic columns. The adjacent Rose Cottage with its twin stone owls atop the gateposts and, like Mary Cottage, a garden well dates from 1826, while Corbiesteps, living up to its name, did not arrive until 1840.

In August 1847 the Danish poet and writer of children's tales, Hans Christian Andersen, then in middle age and on a short visit to Edinburgh, stayed with Joseph Hambro, a member of the banking family whose name has been carried down to modern times in financial circles, at the now demolished Lixmount House which had been built in 1795 by George Andrew, an Edinburgh Writer to the Signet whose wife, Katherine Campbell, had come from the village of Lix in Perthshire. The village gave its name to their house, and the site of Summer Cottage, the former entrance lodge, is marked today by the medical practice located in The Long House, at No. 73 East Trinity Road. In the early years of the 19th century Lixmount belonged to the Farquharsons of Invercauld.

The house known as Christian Bank, pulled down after an existence of only eighty years, was built by the Danish Consul in 1768 and called after King Christian VII of Denmark. In the northern section of Trinity Road, after the opening of the railway line, the site of Christian Bank became the avenue leading to North Trinity House, a gabled and bargeboarded, and now sub-divided, Victorian pile built in 1858 by the architect John Dick Peddie (1824-91) for himself. It carries the monogram PK for his architectural partnership of Peddie & Kinnear. Primrose Bank, the house which gave its name to Primrose Bank Road, still stands opposite the foot of Lomond Road. Built about 1750, it was once the Newhaven Manse and is now called Shirley Lodge. Lomond Road and the streets known as Stirling Road, Lennox Row and Zetland Place are called after ships registered in Leith around 1800.

Towards the sea, on the Laverockbank estate, Sir James Young Simpson (1811-70), whose name is more usually associated with his town residence at No. 52 Queen Street, built the house called Inverforth for his maiden sister. This house, set well back within its garden, still survives. Next door on the southern side, as a country retreat for himself, and because he thought the sea air would be beneficial to his children whose health was a cause for some concern, he bought the 18th century cottage called Viewbank which, together with his considerable additions to it, is now known as Strathavon Lodge. It was here that he hoped eventually to spend his retirement, but the excessive and diverse activities to which his brilliant mind drove him continuously and his many strength-consuming acts of philanthropy, brought his remarkable and

Strathavon Lodge in Laverockbank Road once belonged to Sir James
Young Simpson who had hoped to spend his retirement here.

benevolent life to an end when he was only fifty-nine. Simpson
himself extended the original cottage with what amounted to
a larger house built on at the back and overlooking the sea.
This was further enlarged by the addition of an extra story by
a later owner at the end of the 19th century but, because of
the steeply sloping ground, when seen from the front (or
southern side), all that is visible is the original cottage.

In the garden is the reclining stone 'statue' of a dog traditionally said to represent the one which the doctor used in his
experiments with chloroform. Similar dogs can be found,
however, in at least two other Trinity gardens, and elsewhere

as well, one (painted white) being in front of the Victoria Park Hotel in Ferry Road, and it seems likely that they were simply popular garden ornaments. Simpson's coach-house and stable are still here and the wild garden, with its rough, coarse grass still growing as it did in bygone centuries, is a surviving, virgin fragment of the ancient Wardie Muir. A long, narrow lawn is said to have been Simpson's bowling green. This accords with Cockburn's recollection, mentioned in his *Memorials*, of similar smooth lanes of turf, known as bowling alleys, in the garden of Prestonfield House, the home of his father's friend Sir William Dick of Prestonfield.

William Wilde, Irish father of the more famous Oscar, knew Sir James Simpson well and was, like him, a keen archaeologist and enquirer into natural phenomena. The doctor once asked for his opinion on the placing of a telescope on the roof of Viewbank in pursuance of his amateur astronomical studies, but Wilde successfully discouraged him, maintaining

Recumbent figure of a dog at Strathavon Lodge.

44

that its purpose would be defeated by the Edinburgh weather!

When the name of this historic house was changed it became Strathavon Lodge because Simpson, a native of Bathgate and of Huguenot descent on his mother's side, had chosen to be known as Sir James Young Simpson of Strathavon on receiving his baronetcy. He died at 52 Queen Street in 1870 and was buried in Warriston Cemetery, his family deciding on a last resting place beside that of his children who had predeceased him, although a tomb in Westminster Abbey had been proposed. A portrait medallion was placed there to his memory instead.

On the east side of Laverockbank Road is Starbank Park with flowerbeds, in the shape of a star and two crescent moons, on its sea-facing bank. The Park was created in the later 19th century from the gardens of Laverockbank and Starbank Houses, the Leith architect James Simpson having been employed to lay out the grounds. The demolition of Laverockbank House in 1938 is cause for lamentation. Built as a villa in the early 18th century by a brewing family, a large addition in the form of a long, low range extending beyond each side of the house and containing an oval library was erected along the northern side about a hundred years later. It was approached from the seaward road on the north but the entrance was probably moved to the other, southern, side when the house was enlarged. Not even a lodge remains and Laverockbank Avenue is built across the site.

The house of Starbank was the home of The Rev. Walter M. Goalen who built, at his own expense, the Episcopal chapel later known as Christ Church at the corner of Trinity Road and Primrose Bank Road, the pulpit of which he occupied himself. This graceful little church with its spire among the mature trees which have grown up beside it was designed by John Henderson in 1854 and was a private chapel for twenty or thirty years before being taken over by the Scottish Episcopal Church. It was transformed in recent years into a dwellinghouse, the congregation having united with that of

St. James' at Goldenacre. Starbank House, classically symmetrical in design, is ornamented with neo-Gothic detail and has been converted into two flats for employees of the Parks Department of Edinburgh District Council.

In the spring gales of 1982 the old retaining park wall in Laverockbank Road, its cement no doubt eroded by the frosts of many a severe winter long gone by, was blown down and collapsed in a rickle of stones. The charming old wall has been carefully rebuilt, and it is to be hoped that this will act as a salutary conservation precedent.

Mayville Gardens, a quiet cul-de-sac off Laverockbank Road, was designed in 1881 by J. Hippolyte Blanc and takes its name

Christ Church, Trinity, once a private chapel and now
a private house.

from Mayville in Laverockbank Road, formerly the dower house for Laverockbank House. Large and tall-standing, it has been known as Bankhead for many years and is pleasantly situated next to Starbank Park. Starbank Park House and Bankhead stand directly in line with each other, the later houses in Laverockbank Road lying slightly to the west.

Also in Laverockbank Road is Ivy Cottage, a plain Georgian villa which, renamed Laverock House, was extended on both sides by long corridors and bedrooms in the 1980s to serve as a nursing home. It too has a well within its garden and was for a large part of the present century the home of D. William Kemp of R. Anderson & Co., metal merchants, paint manufacturers and concrete stone makers at 25 and 27 Jane Street in Leith.

Obliquely out of line with the rest of the street, which was built later, is Laverockbank Cottage in the section of East Trinity Road which extends to the east beyond the top of Laverockbank Road. Like Mary Cottage, it has a round, projecting stairtower at the back, a tiny garden at the front and a much larger, walled, garden at the rear. With its deeply oversailing eaves and 'Gothic' doorway, it bears too strong a resemblance to Starbank Park House for this to have been accidental. It is likely that they were both built not only at much the same time but, as many of the Trinity villas were, by the same builder, perhaps George Gunn (of Trinity Mains) who was responsible for Mary Cottage. It is just possible that it was a toll-house and its fortunate survival adds considerably to the interest and character of its surroundings. It was not, however, a lodge at Laverockbank House. The lodge stood further to the east and was demolished many years ago.

In Netherby Road, opposite the west end of Lennox Row, the substantial gates and gate-piers of a former entrance to the grounds of Wardie School have been allowed to remain although no longer required for their original purpose. The main approach to the school has always been from Granton Road. When it was decided to discontinue access from the

Laverockbank Cottage in East Trinity Road bears a strong
resemblance to Starbank Park House, off Laverockbank Road.

eastern side the ground behind the gates was sold when the
gap left in Netherby Road was filled by the building of a
house which is clearly of later' date than those on either side
of it. And it is the newcomer which stands, somewhat self-
consciously, behind the disproportionately large and imposing
gates through which it is entered. Another closed entrance
from Netherby Road can be seen further to the south and
there were originally rights-of-way here from Netherby Road
to Granton Road. (An account of Wardie School and the
Lochinvar Camp built in the school grounds during the
Second World War is given in *Further Traditions of Trinity and
Leith*.)

Starbank House and Park. The house is a larger version of
Laverockbank Cottage and was probably built around the same time.

To the north a group of old houses and cottages in Boswall
Road are deserving of notice. Well back from the street and
hiding among trees stands Earnock, the oldest part of which
was probably built in the 17th century and the newest around
the end of the 19th. Known originally as West Cottage, it was
provided, along with three others, to meet contemporary needs
on the estate of Wardie House. Nearby is the 16th-century
South Cottage, an example of a 'but-and-ben' with an 18th
century extension. East Cottage, which adjoins it, was the
Wardie coach-house, and it is on record that it was once the
home of 'Christopher North'. At the end of Boswall Road
three conjoined houses, Boswall House, with Manor House and

Wardiebank House on either side, form an interesting group. They belonged to Sir Donald Pollock, a former Chancellor of Edinburgh University, who lived in Manor House while the other two became the Pollock Missionary Residences. The external ironwork is also noteworthy as it is said to have come from the liner the *Aquitania* and incorporates an ornamental letter 'A' as well as a trident and crossed anchors in several places. The Cunarder *Aquitania* was completed at John Brown's shipyard on the Clyde in 1914, saw service as a troopship in the First and Second World Wars and carried 1.2 million passengers during a working life of thirty-six years, being taken out of service in 1950. This, however, is a very late date for its ironwork to have been used as railings in Boswall Road. *The Buildings of Scotland: Edinburgh* makes no mention of the liner, referring only to 'monumental front garden walls with extraordinary ironwork'.

The poet and essayist, Alexander Smith, lived in one of the Boswall Road Villas (No. 12, then known as Gesto Villa) and wrote of the great city to which he looked out each morning in his poem *A Vision of Edinburgh as seen from Trinity*. Born at Kilmarnock on 31st December 1829 and the son of a lace pattern designer, he married Flora Macdonald of Skye, 'a blood relation', says his biographer, 'of the Flora Macdonald of unfading romance and fame'. His ultimately death took place on 5th February 1869 and he was buried in Warriston Cemetery where his grave is marked by a Celtic cross with a portrait medallion on the shaft. Also interred in Warriston are Horatio McCulloch, R.S.A., Adam Black the publisher, Sir James Young Simpson, M.D., and Robert Scott Lauder, R.S.A., one of Scotland's most outstanding 19th century painters whose tomb bears a medallion portrait sculpted by J. Hutchinson, R.S.A.

Boswall Road is not, strictly speaking, in Trinity but in Wardie which has its own church on a corner site in Primrose Bank Road the history of which was written for the centenary of the church by Dr W.S. Robertson. 'In 1885', he writes in

Wardie Church 1885–1985, 'Wardie was still open ground. The name "Trinity" was confined to the narrow strip of land on each side of Trinity Road' and the 'eighteenth century mansions, such as Trinity Lodge and Trinity Grove, had been joined by a mere handful of new villas', while there 'was a working and fishing community in the Duke of Buccleuch's cottages east and west of Granton Harbour'. This was therefore not a highly populated area and such residents as there were were more than adequately provided with places of worship. It did not, however, have a United Presbyterian Church and the initiative to have one built was taken by James Fleming, an elder in Bonnington U.P. Church 'a mile and a half away'.

Born in 1833 in Balerno and the son of a shepherd, James Fleming had established himself in a prosperous business in Edinburgh and lived in the still extant but at that time isolated Dalmore Lodge in Trinity Road.

Reservations about the desirability of building a U.P. church in Wardie having been with difficulty overcome by Fleming, the new congregation first met for worship in May 1885 in Bayton Terrace (as the few houses which had been built by that time in Granton Road were called). 'The 58 members of 1885' however were to 'become 200 by the end of 1891' and as early as July 1885 they moved to a wooden hall and vestry 'on the site of the present church'. The following year James Fleming himself met the cost of a stone-built hall (the present church hall) but suffered a 'financial disaster' from which it took him several years to recover, at which time he nevertheless resumed his generosity to the church.

Finally, on 5th November 1893, after a period of vigorous fund-raising – 'the people laboured in the task for many years' – Wardie Church was opened with provision for 500 members. The Rev. A. Ian Dunlop in *The Kirks of Edinburgh 1560–1984* describes it as 'a traditional, rectangular building with pitched tile roof, a small tower at the roof centre and two turrets at the northern end. The ceiling is round-vaulted and there are galleries on three sides.' The architect was John McLachlan. It had cost £5000 which included £470 for the organ. Above the door is carved a dove with an olive leaf, the symbol of the United Presbyterian Church. 'With no houses round about, the building must', says Dr Robertson, 'have been a conspicuous landmark.'

The first minister was The Rev. James Macleod, 'an energetic, wise and thoughtful pastor', who died at the age of forty-seven in 1907, 'a few days after the death of James Fleming'.

Now surrounded by well-populated streets and with an enthusiastic Church of Scotland congregation, Wardie Church carries forward its old traditions of worship, witness and service into the future.

Wardie Square, stretching west from Wardie Steps and which is far from being square, dates from around 1840, Wardie Hotel, in Lower Granton Road, was built in 1881 and, further to the west, East Cottages have formed a long, red-brick row since c. 1840. Further west still Granton Square, designed by William Burn in 1838, contains, says *Edinburgh: An Illustrated Architectural Guide* 1992, 'imposing buildings associated with the Duke of Buccleuch's development of Granton Harbour including' the former Granton Inn, with a portico of twin Roman Doric columns, which is now H.M.S. Claverhouse, Forth Division, R.N.R.

Wardie House, already mentioned as one of the two subjects of my 'mad March morning' conversation, was the successor to the ancient Wardie Castle which witnessed the disembarkation of Hertford's troops in 1544. The original building date is not known but was probably some time during the early 16th century and it was rebuilt after becoming ruinous in the 18th century, this new building being itself reconstructed in 1860. It contained, in the oldest part of the building, a low-ceilinged room known as the Cromwell Room, though whether the tradition that the Lord Protector of the Commonwealth and son of a Huntingdon farmer (1599–1658) actually 'slept here' is far from certain. (It is possible that, as already noted, the use of stones from the old castle to build the Citadel in Leith may have given rise to this belief.) The room, which may only have dated from the early 1700s, has been described as being 'painted with the crests of England and Scotland' and the date 1649 had been scratched under a stained glass window. Two crests and two views of Edinburgh were shown in this window. The views were believed to be copies of engravings by De Witt and to have portrayed the Castle and 'Edinburgh from the river'. One crest was the Scottish coat-of-arms but the other could not be identified.

The house, for which the rent was once 'part of a pair of gilt spurs', was owned in the 18th century by Sir Alexander Boswall who was also the owner of Blackadder House near Duns in Berwickshire which was latterly a ruin. And in the early 19th century it was occupied by an atiquary who discovered a Bronze Age urn in the vicinity which he presented to the Museum of Antiquities in Queen Street.

By the 1820s the house was owned by a family called Yule who built the most recent additions, including the tower. Their crest was carved over the door and painted on the ceilings and fireplace tiles.

Consumed by dry rot which 'crumbled its flooring, warped its panelling, cracked its walls and sagged its painted ceilings', Wardie House had reached the point of no return by 1955 when, except for the surviving turreted fragment in its little front garden, it was pulled down. There was at one time a cast-iron dog kennel in the garden and the mark left on the wall to which it was attached can still be seen.

The other, and neighbouring, substantial house in Wardie is Challenger Lodge, formerly Wardie Lodge, the history of which is given in Chapter 3.

Coal, though not of a very high quality, was mined in Wardie (one pit which, because of wildfire, had to be abandoned was known as 'Weirdy Pit') and cottars gathered coal on Wardie shore. Remnants of old pits have been found at

Wardie House in 1955, before demolition. The original caption read:
'Wardie House is "falling down" – tower demolished, slates removed,
the house makes a sad picture after its long history and days of
grandeur' (*Photograph courtesy Scotsman Publications Ltd.*).

Royston and it is known that in 1788 a pit was sunk in Pilton
Wood. Had it not been for its development for dwellinghouses,
the area might have become the scene of unrestricted open-
cast coalmining. As well as mining, the Salt Springs of Wardie
in the Forth gave rise to the salt pans here.

Dwellinghouses also cover the site of Wardie Farm which
was in existence at 11 Rosebank Road until 1947.

The Victorian predilection for cottages no doubt prompted
the retention of the name of Trinity Cottage (there had previously been a cottage on the site) for the tall, baronial-type
mansion built on the southern flank of Trinity at Goldenacre
(once known, because of its fertility in contrast to the stub-
born, unproductive moor, as Goldenriggs) as recently as 1894
by the Leith shipowning, family of Currie. The house was used
as the business premises of their shipping line after the death
of the original Mr Currie in 1943. Architecturally, Trinity

Trinity Cottage at Goldenacre in the Spring of 1969 shortly before its demolition. It had been the home of the Currie family who founded the Currie Line.

Cottage looked backward to an earlier Scottish building style (like the picturesque row of riverside almshouses, of identical date and medieval in conception down to the commemorative donor's tablet on the street-facing gable, at Coltbridge) rather than forward to the space-age, synthetic functionalism that was to work out its urban destiny in the 20th century.

The original cottage is marked on some 19th century maps of the district. Around 1830 it was the home of the farmer at Windlestrawlee a short distance to the west in Ferry Road. The subsequent mansionhouse, rearing its crow-stepped heights among trees that were noted for their age and beauty, rose grandly above a well-kept hedge to look out, in spring, on a carpet of lush grass and crocuses.

It was a high, cold old house, as a descendant of the Currie family wrote in 1968, recalling her memories of the 1920s, with a long drawing-room and a huge fireplace, which could accommodate yard-long logs, in a room at the top of the building. When her great-aunt, who lived there latterly alone with a 'kind, sandy -haired maid who stood like a grenadier in her white cap and apron', died, the mansion became a home for babies waiting for adoption, remaining so until the evacuation of the children during World War II and the transfer from Leith of the Currie Line Offices (an independent shipping company from 1836–1969). The gardens of Trinity Cottage and the turreted, dormer-windowed Larkfield were opened to the public from 2 to 7 p.m. on Sunday, 13th May 1952 – admission one shilling (5p) – in aid of the Scottish Queen's Nurses' Benevolent and Educational Funds and the Gardens Committee of The National Trust for Scotland.

Larkfield, on the west side of the estate and entered from Wardie Road, was an older house than Trinity Cottage. Although of secondary importance after the advent of the larger building, it was of considerable interest and was rebuilt to the designs of the architect Hippolyte Blanc in the late 19th century, its red roofs contrasting with the more sombre-looking later house.

Thanks to the onward march of progress, these two houses were demolished in 1969 and the beautiful small estate has been redeveloped. The half-timbered, English-style lodge at the entrance to Larkfield in Wardie Road was occupied for a time by an architectural practice and it looked as though it (and its mature garden) might be allowed to survive, but it too has gone, replaced by a block of flats behind the gate-piers where 'Larkfield' can still be seen cut into the stone. A few trees were permitted to remain along with the Trinity Cottage gates and lodge opposite Inverleith Row, but as for the rest – like the gowk, redevelopers hae nae sang but ane! The curving

The house of Larkfield, which stood near the former Trinity Cottage at Goldenacre, when the grounds were open to the public in April 1952 (*Photograph courtesy Scotsman Publications Ltd.*).

walls of Trinity Park House, occupied as Government offices, now spread their artstone banality across the site.

Nonetheless, Trinity (a designated conservation area) remains remarkably unspoiled in comparison with other places and, if Scott and Constable and the brothers Ballantyne could walk today down the streets they knew so well, they would probably be well able to recognise it, although they would find its rural character greatly changed. An aura of history, and the individuality of the Georgian and Victorian houses and, in large measure also, their gardens, make it still one of the most charming and, in the language of the estate agents, desirable residential districts of the city in spite of the inevitable intrusion of some new building (by no means to be wholly discouraged) into the area, not all of which, however, has been designed to blend with its environment. Above all, the infilling of Wardie Bay, with its disastrous consequences, has (it is to be hoped permanently) been avoided.

The house called Newbank lay (in South Trinity Road) immediately to the north of Trinity Cottage and the disused railway line, and beyond it was the more extensive ground of Rose Park, with its Georgian villa well away from the street. In 1962 Rose Park was auctioned by Dowells (now Phillips Scotland) of George Street along with 1.6 acres of land for building purposes. As so often happens, all that remained (until taken down in 1985) was the gate-piered entrance with the name 'Rose Park' still readable in fading white-painted lettering on one of the stones. (This particular stone was rescued and has been preserved inside the Rose Park housing complex off South Trinity Road.)

Round the corner in East Trinity Road, Mayfield House has the distinction of having been the home of Christian Salvesen. As a young Norwegian only sixteen years of age he came to Scotland to enter a shipbroking firm in Glasgow. After spending some time in Germany and his native country, he returned to Edinburgh in 1851 and joined his brother in the

The Georgian house of Rosepark, before its demolition in 1962, in South Trinity Road (*Photograph courtesy Scotsman Publications Ltd.*).

business of Salvesen & Turnbull. His own shipping concern, Christian Salvesen & Co., came later and three of his sons, all born in Leith, went into their father's employment there. A fourth son became Lord Salvesen, a Senator of the College of Justice. Christian Salvesen died in Mayfield House in January 1911, aged 83, and was buried in Rosebank Cemetery.

Mayfield House, which consists of ground and first floors above a basement, and contains a panelled billiard room, was built in the mid-19th century. It was used as a hospital during both World Wars and after the former was run as a home for the orphaned sons of naval personnel. In 1959 the house was given to The Leonard Cheshire Foundation when it was opened as the first Cheshire Home in Scotland, a chapter in its history which may come to an end before long as Mayfield, and the residential additions which had been made to the house, was offered for sale, together with its gardens, in 1995.

The house of Denham Green in Clark Road was given by

Mayfield House in East Trinity Road from the west. Latterly a Cheshire Home, its future is presently undecided.

the Salvesens to the Edinburgh Academy and served for years as its Junior Preparatory School. Sold to a builder by the Academy, however, in 1987, it and its grounds have been replaced by modern flats. On John Ainslie's map of 1804 Denham Green is shown as the property of The Rev. Sir Henry Moncrieff Wellwood, who had bought it in 1798, when it was called Bangholm. He changed the name, although the reason is not recorded. It was a residence of the Earl of Caithness in the 1830s.

In the angle between Mayfield House and the former Denham Green House, Earl Haig Gardens can be reached by the approach path on the south side of East Trinity Road. This First World War Settlement was one of many established by the Scottish Veterans' Garden City Association for disabled ex-servicemen and their families and the site was obtained by the Leith Committee from the Salvesens, a gift which considerably curtailed their own grounds. Thirty-one flatted villas were then built round a central square, Field Marshall Earl Haig performing the opening ceremony on 1st October 1921, an event recorded on an inscribed stone at the entrance in East Trinity Road. Carved tablets can be seen on some of the houses commemorating the sons of many families, including the Salvesens, who fell in action. On a wet July day in 1923 the Settlement was visited by King George V and Queen Mary when a special pavilion was put up for their official reception. After touring the houses and talking with the men and their wives and children, the Queen planted a tree in a corner of the square to mark the occasion.

Returning to East Trinity Road, the usual remnant of an entrance gate was left standing when Trinity House, a central block with later, 19th-century, additions on either side, was demolished in 1978. It had belonged to Dunbar, the funeral directors, who had their stabling (later garageing) here also, and the last owner was the House of Fraser. The proliferation of modern houses now occupying the site is in stark contrast to the beautiful Georgian dwellings behind their long-established walls and gardens on the other side, such as Rose Cottage with its stone-carved owls perpetually perched in imminent flight already mentioned.

These individually-designed houses of exceptional merit are equalled in distinction in Lennox Row by Grecian Cottage and by Gothic House round the corner in York Road, and here also is the high-standing and far-viewing Lomond House poised above the clifftop where twin arches lead to it and, on the southern side, to Forthland House which, together with Holly Lodge at No. 18, have long been the two residential homes for the elderly run by the Leith Benevolent Association.

Lomond House stands at the slope's top in York Road and looks out across the Firth of Forth.

The feuing of ground at what is today Laverockbank Road began about 1835, although the short line of terraced villas, with gardens, at the south-east end was not continued further as originally intended. But the history of Laverockbank goes back much further than this. In 1660 a Leith wine merchant, brewer and landowner called Maurice Trent bought land here from the Crown and called it Larkbank. Then in 1748 it was purchased by the Leith wine cooper Patrick Anderson who renamed it Laverockbank. 'Laverock is but lark writ large' and both versions of the name reflect the large numbers of these little songbirds which, we are told, 'came hither in snow', though it is many a long year since their song was heard. They were sold in Newhaven, along with the fish, as delicacies for the table and were fortuitously saved from that fate when their habitat was taken over by the villa builders. The birds are said to have 'migrated to the Solway', but wherever they may have gone their name, as euphonious as their song, is all that remains in Trinity as their memorial. In 1761 the eastern section of the bank was acquired by nurserymen, detached from Laverockbank and given the name of Cherry Bank.

The house on the corner of East Trinity and Laverockbank Roads (and next door to Woodville of which an account is given in Chapter 5) provides an example of the vicissitudes which individual dwellinghouses can experience. Built around 1816 as a single-storey cottage, it was enlarged by the addition of an upper floor about seventy years later and can be traced on old maps as having started life as a nameless 'cottage', going on to become successively Spring Cottage, Ramsay Cottage and then The Cottage. Finally, following conversion to upper and lower flats at the end of the Second World War, it ended up with two separate street numbers in Laverockbank Road (the original entrance) and East Trinity Road (the entrance to the upper flat). Part of the garden was lost when the pavement was widened in the 1930s, probably at the same time as it was widened at Hay Lodge. The house, when Ramsay Cottage, was owned by the Rev. George R. Davidson in 1876, by J. C.

The house formerly known as The Cottage at the corner of
Laverockbank Road c. 1910.

The same house after post-war conversion to upper and lower flats.

Deans (who changed the name to The Cottage) in 1886, by
W. A. Young in 1889 and then by my great-grandfather Young
Johnston Pentland, a Leith Town Councillor and Bailie, the
story of whose family is to be found in *Further Traditions of
Trinity and Leith*. The Cottage and Woodville are not men-
tioned in the Post Office Directories until after Laverock
Bank had become Laverockbank Road in 1872.

Charles A. Christianson, of Scandinavian origin and a
flour and produce merchant at No. 26 Bernard Street and 45
and 47 Timber Bush in Leith, had his house at No. 3
Laverockbank Road in the Georgian terrace opposite
Woodville.

A blocked-up doorway in the wall north of Laverockbank
Grove may have been an entrance to the demolished house
called The Grove the place of which has been taken by the
modern Roseville Gardens houses. Around 1900 it was the
home of James Waldie, of the old-established family of coal
merchants with offices in Leith and Edinburgh. The last occupants were called Lorimer, owners of the Trinity Laundry in
Hawthornvale.

Andrew Jeffrey, in his book *This Present Emergency:
Edinburgh, The River Forth and South-East Scotland During the
Second World War*, published in 1992, writes of shrapnel falling
in Granton, Portobello and other parts of the city during an
air raid in 1939. 'Potentially lethal shell caps', he says, 'made
of brass and lead were crashing to earth. One fell in the front
garden at 24 Laverockbank Avenue and damaged a concrete
path.' It was 'still hot when handed to a passing policeman
some minutes later'!

As interesting examples of the wide variety of architectural
styles indulged in in Victorian times, Gothic House in York
Road and Grecian Cottage in Lennox Row have been already
mentioned, as has also Lomond House standing proud on
its commanding height with a fashionable tower ensuring for
its owners an uninterrupted view well beyond the Lomond
Hills. There are gables, imitation English-style half-timbering,

Gothic House, one of many interestingly designed houses
in 19th century Trinity.

romantic cottages, like Heatherlie in East Trinity Road, that
have grown as greater space was needed into substantial
houses, and gate lodges and little carriage drives as well.
Pretentious? At the time perhaps, but what a rare environmental legacy for the generations that were to come!

A little rustic building known as Goldenacre Cottage stood
for many years on the south-east side of South Trinity Road,
but this has long since disappeared.

Trinity had its own railway station, entered from York
Road where housebuilding operations in recent years have
obliterated all that remained of it on that side. After the closure

of the station it could be approached from Trinity Crescent, but the ground here has been enclosed as gardens for the householders in the former railway buildings, now adapted to residential use, to which access is still obtained by the old entrance in York Road. The line of the railway (a single line the rails of which have now been removed) still passes straight as a die across the old lands of Warriston. From Ferry Road, under which it runs, it can be seen approaching from the south between the east end of Heriot's Playing Fields and the west end of the new housing enclave of Easter Warriston, and then, to the north, continuing its straight course towards the former Trinity Station. That part of the track between the station buildings and the north end of Trinity Road has been remade as a narrow road (for pedestrians and cyclists only).

The trains left Canal Street Station, on the site of the later Waverley Station carriage entrance on Waverley Bridge, and were run downhill through a tunnel to Scotland Street Station (and cable-hauled uphill in the opposite direction). From there some of them went, running about every quarter of an hour, to Bonnington and then to North Leith Station at the Citadel, and others were detached and run to Trinity and Granton where they caught the Fife Ferry (a specially constructed boat, with rails on to which the trains could run, called the *Leviathan*) which merits a place in history as the world's first train ferry service. The Scotland Street Tunnel route was closed in 1868 on the opening of a new line through Abbey-hill to Bonnington and Trinity. It had only been in use for about twenty years, but as it passed beneath Drummond Place in the Second New Town it had necessitated the demolition of the Georgian mansion of Bellevue, by then the Excise Office, because of the danger of subsidence.

The district also had its own masonic lodge, Lodge Trinity No. 885, founded in the closing years of the 19th century in purpose-built premises at the foot of Wardie Road. Many local functions were held here, including the annual dances of the still extant Lomond Park Tennis Club which played a prominent part in the social life of Trinity in the years before the First World War. The Lodge, vacated by the freemasons who now meet elsewhere, has been redesigned for residential purposes, and thus another chapter of Trinity history has been brought to an end.

Tradition and local characters persisted in Trinity, as in other places, into the early years of the 20th century. Prior to 1914 the aged Russian Consul to the Port of Leith, who lived in Lennox Row, was often to be seen pacing up and down the pavement beside his gardan wall and carrying a stool so that he could sit down periodically for a rest outside his gate! A few four-in-hands and carriages were still in use by some families, including the Salvesens of Mayfield House in East Trinity Road and the Sandersons of Trinity House (also in East Trinity Road and pulled down and redeveloped in 1978) who drove out in their carriage with a groom at the back blowing a horn as they travelled through the Edinburgh streets in style. Newbank in South Trinity Road, the home of a son of Sir Richard Mackie, was one of the last houses where a dog-cart, very smart and with brightly painted wheels, was kept. A Dalmation dog used to run behind it, as the custom was, when out on the road.

Troughs for watering the tradesmen's and cab-drivers' hard-working animals were a common sight as well, as also, less fortunately, were fallen horses, especially in winter when sacks were usually placed on icy roads for them to stand on when pulled up.

Colourful and stylish, these times have come and gone, and probably the least changing feature in the landscape is the old Edenburgh Fyrth itself – forby the Edinburgh weather!

'What a dreadful day!', said a passer-by on the pavement, holding her umbrella squarely into a squall. 'Terrible!', I replied, and took a firmer grip of the camera, now replete with scenes of azure skies and the sun-drenched stones of Trinity. Then the March wind caught the dark, bare, winter

The old walls and trees of Laverockbank Road where it slopes
steeply towards the sea.

branches of the trees and shook them roundly, as if impatient
for the first green hint of leaves: and suddenly the sun blazed
out across the brown earth rich with snowdrops in the gardens,
and for a few bright moments it was Spring.

CHAPTER THREE

The Story of Challenger Lodge

The house behind the high retaining wall, set down, a diminutive stately home, in some seclusion on the north side of Boswall Road has a long and interesting history. It was built in 1825 (the architect is unknown but it may possibly have been to the design of William Henry Playfair (1790–1857), one of the architects of the New Town) and the grounds around it were laid out for Dr Thomas Hope, a bachelor who was Professor of Chemistry and Pharmacy at the University of Edinburgh, and who, in his leisure hours, indulged his own predilection for the growing of plants. He then installed his niece Frances, the daughter of his brother James Hope, W.S., in Wardie Lodge, the name given to her elegant, single-storeyed new home with its pedimented Greek Doric portico supported on four columns, its entrance hall surmounted by a circular Georgian cupola and its magnificent views of the Firth of Forth from the rear windows. Known locally, of old, as 'the sea captains' terrace', Boswall Road, because of its situation, was a place of residence favoured by ships' captains from the port of Leith.

The family of Miss Frances Jane Hope was descended from Sir Thomas Hope of Craighall (1573–1646), Lord, or, as the office was known then, King's Advocate under Charles I. Hopetoun House at South Queensferry was also built by an earlier generation of his descendants. Sir Thomas's great-great-grandson was the botanist Dr John Hope (1725–86) and he it was who successfully transferred the two physic gardens, the Royal Abbey Garden at Holyrood and the Town Garden on a site now covered by the Waverley Station, to the north side of Haddington Place where the combined gardens became known as the Leith Walk Botanic Garden, in 1763. It remained there until 1820 when, as already noted, it was finally moved to Inverleith. As Dr John Hope was the grandfather of Frances Jane, or Fanny as she was usually called, it can therefore be no mere coincidence that she became a pioneer natural gardener at Wardie Lodge. Her father, James Hope, W.S. (rather confusingly, he had the same name as his father who was also a Writer to the Signet), the brother of Dr Thomas Hope who had built Wardie Lodge, was legal adviser to Thomas Telford and carried out the large amount of conveyancing work required for his road- and bridge-building enterprises. He is mentioned by A. R. B. Haldane in the preface to his book *New Ways Through the Glens*. Less well known than his definitive work on *The Drove Roads of Scotland*, it gives an account of the roads and bridges constructed in the Scottish Highlands by General Wade and Thomas Telford.

As a horticulturist Fanny specialised in trees and shrubs, and also in coloured kale, of which she had a spectacular winter border, and hellebores in a gardening experiment that placed flowers and kitchen garden vegetables together in a layout that was later adopted in England by Gertrude Jekyll, who was slightly younger than Miss Hope. Together with her gardeners, and working long and energetic hours herself, she carried out what has been called her 'quiet revolution' in gardening at Wardie Lodge that soon acquired a well-deserved reputation for the number of rare and exotic shrubs which thrived in that 'mild and sunny spot' and in her greenhouses.

Though largely neglected today, Fanny's work was widely recognised during her lifetime and, as well as her own visits to many other famous gardens in Scotland and England, she had frequent calls at Wardie Lodge alike from distinguished enquirers and the noted experts of the time. She was, nevertheless, of a quiet and retiring disposition, choosing writing as the means of passing on her skill and knowledge, and her articles in the *Gardeners' Chronicle* during the 1860s and '70s can still be read today, as also can her book, *Notes and Thoughts on Gardens and Woodlands*, published in 1881, a copy of which is held by the Edinburgh Room of the Central Public Library.

With her natural aptitude for flower arranging, it is no surprise to learn that her drawing-room, with its large windows overlooking the sea, was never without its imaginative adornments of flowers-of-the-field and leaves and mosses mixed with choice exotics and rare greenhouse plants. She was also mindful of the deprived, of which there were many in her day, whose lives were spent in the mean streets and tenements of the city and arranged for her posies of sweet-smelling flowers and herbs from her garden to be sent to the houses of the poor and distributed in the wards of the Edinburgh Royal Infirmary. This was the day of the 'flower missions' when local newspapers carried appeals to garden owners to share their bounty with the hospital and the poorhouse where a welcome touch of beauty and colour must have brightened many a drab and cheerless life.

Frances Hope died at Wardie Lodge, at a fairly advanced age, on 26th April 1880. An example of the influence she exerted is the extent to which her garden designs, themselves harking back to the gardens of Scotland in the 17th century, were taken as models by Sir Robert Lorimer when engaged in the restoration of some of the country's major houses and castles and their grounds. When recalling his work at the 16th century mansion of Earlshall in Fife in 1891 Lorimer wrote: 'Such surprises – little gardens within the garden, the "month's" garden, the herb garden, the yew alley. The kitchen garden, too, – and this nothing to be ashamed of, to be smothered away from the house, but made delightful by its laying out.'

After her death the house remained in the possession of the Hope family until it was bought, in 1887 or 1888, by Lieutenant-General Sir John McLeod, G.C.B., who had formerly been Commander-in-Chief of Ceylon. His son, Brigadier

N.M. McLeod, wrote in 1953 that, although he believed the younger of Miss Hope's gardeners (the last two of whom, father and son, had been known successively as 'Old MacIntyre') had stayed on, his father 'did away with some of the shrubberies to make lawns and flower beds in which he took a great pride.' He recalled having spent ten of the happiest years of his life, between the ages of two and twelve, 'at Wardie Lodge, now Challenger Lodge Home', and he continued, 'I need hardly say that for us three boys and our friends it was "Paradise", and to know that the dear old place provides healing and happiness to so many less fortunate children would, I am sure, give great satisfaction to all former inhabitants. Sir John Murray bought the property in 1897, changing the name to Challenger Lodge, but I rejoice to see that the old name is still discernible on the gate posts.' This is no longer to be seen, however, as the name has been altered to Challenger Lodge at the entrance in Boswall Road.

Before it became the home for the 'less fortunate children' mentioned by Brigadier McLeod, Wardie Lodge was purchased in 1897 (or, according to Dr W.N. Boog Watson, in 1898) from his father by one of the most outstanding men of the late 19th century in Edinburgh, John, later Sir John, Murray, K.C.B., F.R.S., LL.D., D.Sc. With his family, he removed from the centre of Edinburgh to the little classical mansion by the sea, on which he had spent more years of his life than on dry land, when Wardie Lodge became a meeting place for men of learning from around the world who knew the worth and achievements of 'Murray of the Challenger'.

John Murray (1841–1914), the son of an accountant, was born in Cobourg, Ontario, in Canada, and attended school initially in that country but, coming to Scotland in 1858 for the completion of his education, was a pupil at the High School in Stirling and, finally, a student at Edinburgh University. Qualifying as a marine naturalist, he visited Spitzbergen and the Arctic region on a whaling ship in 1868 and it was this experience, when he was aged twenty-seven, that set a pattern for the future and established his lifelong interest in oceanography. In 1889 he married Isabel Henderson, whose father was a shipowner, and they had two sons and three daughters who were sent, as young children, to Miss Yule's School in Trinity.

The voyage, and the editing of the subsequent Report, for which he became well-known during his lifetime was the Challenger Expedition organised by the University of Edinburgh and led by Sir Wyville Thomson, Professor of Zoology in that University, during the years 1872–76. This study of the ocean basins of the world took the 2306-ton steam corvette HMS Challenger, with its own laboratories on board, to the Atlantic, the Indian and the Pacific Oceans sailing from Sheerness in December 1872 and returning, having covered over seventy thousand miles, to Spithead in May 1876, thus completing the greatest oceanographic voyage in history at that time.

Sir Wyville was appointed Director of the Commission responsible for classifying the specimens and records collected during these explorations. On his early death in 1882 he was succeeded as Director of that Commission by John Murray who then took over the compiling and editing of the massive *Report on the Scientific Results of the Voyage of H.M.S. Challenger*, a task which took years of painstaking and unremitting work between 1880 and 1895 and for which he was subsequently knighted. The Report was published by the Stationery Office in fifty volumes and included, in addition to a Narrative of the Cruise, sections on such diverse studies as Botany, Chemistry, Zoology, Deep Sea Deposits and many others. In the Introduction to the Narrative of the Cruise the origins of oceanography are traced back to the late 15th century when 'The rage for geographical exploration which set in after the discovery of America naturally brought the phenomena of the sea into greater prominence.' Quoting the biographer of Sir John Hawkins, the Elizabethan sailor who was knighted for his services against the Spanish Armada, it continues, 'Were it not for the Moving of the Sea, by the Force of Winds, Tides and Currents, it would corrupt all the World.'

This dedicated and intrepid ocean explorer was also the founder of the first marine station for scientific research in Great Britain which was opened in Edinburgh at Granton Point in 1884, and for this venture Challenger Lodge provided him with a conveniently situated residence. The station was equipped with a floating laboratory and a steam yacht which was used for dredging and taking soundings. The yacht was called the *Medusa* and in it he and his assistants explored the coastal waters around the shores of Scotland.

To enable him more readily to carry out this work Sir John brought his scientific material and his technical staff to premises which he had acquired on the other, south, side of Boswall Road which consisted of a villa, stables and a garden cottage. This time it was his yacht which inspired the choice of name and the property then became known as Villa Medusa. Later, after Sir John Murray's time, the house was called Medusa Cottage and this name can be seen at the present day at the entrance to the former villa which, along with the original cottage and stables, has been superseded by a modern house which has taken over the old name.

In addition to his research work at Granton Point, John Murray tirelessly carried out a bathymetrical survey of Scottish freshwater lochs between 1897 and 1909, he leased, explored and financed expeditions to Christmas Island and, in 1910, he explored the North Atlantic. Oceanic interests were dominant even on a recreational level, yachting being one of his favourite pursuits and also the study of marine deposits of which he had a large collection. His published works include *On the Origin and Structure of Coral Reefs and Islands* dated 1880. But he did not die at sea, nor, indeed, in Challenger Lodge. By a great misfortune he was killed instantaneously in a motor accident in 1914.

It was fitting that honour was paid to this illustrious, if adopted, son of Edinburgh at the Second International

Congress on the History of Oceanography on the centenary of the Challenger Expedition, in Edinburgh in 1972, when eminent scientists from around the world attended its meetings. An exhibition was also mounted by the Royal Scottish Museum in Chambers Street between 8th July and 24th September.

In the years 1915 and 1916 Challenger Lodge was still functioning as the Challenger Expedition Office and Lake Survey with James Chumley as Secretary, located in Villa Medusa, also stated in the Post Office Directories for these years to be the 'Challenger Expedition Office, Boswall Road'. In 1917 this information is repeated but the name and title of the secretary do not appear. During these years Lady Murray's name is given as well, but in 1918 the only entry is 'Lady Murray, Challenger Lodge', by which year the Expedition Office would therefore seem to have been closed down. In 1885, during the period in which the Challenger Report was being written and compiled, the Directory states that the 'Challenger Expedition Commission' was at No. 32 Queen Street.

Lady Murray, Sir John's widow, was still resident in the house in 1919 and 1920 but there is no entry for her or for Challenger Lodge in 1921. In 1922 the information given is 'United Service Children's Home, Challenger Lodge', an entry which is repeated until 1928. After the departure of Lady Murray the Lodge was not again occupied as a family home. Villa Medusa is not recorded throughout the post-Expedition Office years but it reappears later as Medusa Cottage, e.g. in 1938 when it was occupied by 'Charles Frederick Smyth, engineer'. It is possible that for a time its name may have been changed again, as has happened in the case of numerous other Edinburgh houses. The Challenger Society was subsequently founded in England for the Promotion of the Study of Oceanography.

Interest and incident however continued to cling, ivy-like, to the ageing but still sound and serviceable walls of Challenger

Lodge. Its character had now been changed to that of a caring and hospitable institution, thereby setting a precedent for the future down to, and doubtless well beyond, the late 20th century. In 1929 it was acquired by The Edinburgh Cripple and Invalid Children's Aid Society when it became home to about forty boys and girls, many of whom were suffering from infantile paralysis, usually referred to now as 'polio'. Here the children were well looked after and as much remedial work as could be done was carried out. As time passed, however, it became increasingly clear that one of the most important facilities for relieving this and other incapacitating conditions and for enhancing the health of the children committed to the Society's care would be the one thing they lacked, a curative

The cupola above the entrance hall at Challenger Lodge.

hydrotherapy pool. And it was not until 1936 that this pressing need was met after the death of Mrs Dorothy Troup
whose sympathetic concern for the work being undertaken at
Challenger Lodge extended over many years. In the summer
of that year the longed-for pool was opened by her husband,
Mr G. E. Troup of the Scottish Juvenile Welfare and After-Care
Office at 11 Manor Place, who had organised and financed its
construction in memory of his wife whose 'love for and devo-
tion to the interests of the crippled children was referred to
by several speakers at the function and whose great desire had
been that they should have such a pool.' They found it difficult, they said, to articulate what her loss would mean to the
Home. Appreciation was also expressed by the Matron, Miss
Thomson. After the ceremony the visitors saw some of the
children enjoying the warm water of the new pond, which
permitted much more effective remedial work to be attempted,
'while other children had tea in the garden and a few bolder
spirits were actually using the swings.'

Less active amusements were provided for under a marquee.
The event was reported in the Edinburgh newspapers which
included a photograph of the children with some of the nurses
in the water.

The pool was built of reinforced concrete lined with tiles
and 'the floor of the pond hall laid with Moulmein teak',
while the roof was entirely of glass. The whole memorial was
designed and supervised by J. Rochead-Williamson, F.R.I.A.S.

In March 1962 'a very special film star' made his home at
the Lodge in the quarters reserved for the children's pets. This
was the dog, a three-year-old Skye terrier, which had taken the
part of Greyfriars Bobby in the Walt Disney film of that name
and, while filming was taking place, a value of one hundred
thousand pounds had been placed on this little latter-day
portrayer of the original and faithful Bobby who lay on his
master's grave in Greyfriars Churchyard until his own turn
came to be buried there beside him.

The arrangements for him to be given to Challenger Lodge

were made by Chief Constable William Merrilees of Lothians and Peebles Police, the children's much-loved 'Uncle Willie' and a well-known figure in the city in the recent past. The idea had occurred to him when Bobby was taken to meet the children by a director of Walt Disney productions who was in Edinburgh in 1961 for the premier of the film, and his help was enlisted to allow Bobby to be given a home among the young residents who already had two cats, two rabbits, a poodle, a tortoise and a 'budgie'. It is on record that Bobby settled down happily beside his new companions.

The Home was wholly dependent on voluntary contributions and charitable donations and, by 1954, it was 'living on capital which reflected sadly on public generosity, a state which could not continue without its very existence being endangered.' The number of children had now fallen to twenty-five. They managed to keep going, however, until 1975 when, forty-six years after opening its doors, Challenger Lodge was closed and the remaining fifteen children transferred to Graysmill School for physically handicapped children run by Edinburgh Corporation.

A new role was quickly found for the old house in Boswall Road, when, soon after the departure of the disabled children, it was bought, in May 1975, for the purpose for which it is now being used. The interior was badly in need of renovation and repair but it still stood, its classical elegance mellowed and matured by the stirring and eventful earlier years down which it had travelled, awaiting and inviting within its portals its next occupants. Its vacation coincided with the search being made in the mid-1970s for suitable premises in which to open a hospice for the terminally ill in Edinburgh and a decision to purchase Challenger Lodge was made when the attractions of the house, the garden and the outstanding seaside situation had overcome concern about the amount of work which would require to be carried out within it. So, in December 1977, after two and a half years of hard work, concentrated fund-raising and, as it was later proved to be, justifiable optimism, the doors behind the stately Doric columns were again flung welcomingly open to admit those who, sadly, stood in need of the skill, the unfailing care and the Christian love which were soon to be recognised as the hallmarks of St. Columba's Hospice.

On Sunday, 12th December 1982, in celebration of its fifth anniversary, a service was held in St. Andrew's and St. George's Church in George Street and this was followed by a visit to Challenger Lodge by Lord Provost Tom Morgan and the Lady Provost who met and chatted with the patients during a tour of the Hospice. The tenth anniversary service was held in the High Kirk of St. Giles when Mrs Eleanor McLaughlin, the Lord Provost and one of the Patrons of the Hospice, was present. Mrs McLaughlin has shown a great interest in the work of St. Columba's which she has visited on several occasions.

The story of its work, of the dedication of many people which led to its establishment and of the additional buildings which have since been erected in the grounds was interestingly and movingly told in 1991 in *Letting Go and Living* by Yvonne Bostock. Among these additional buildings was a new nursing wing (which increased the number of patients to thirty as opposed to fifteen when the Hospice opened) and for this development the hydrotherapy pool was filled in and built over in 1980. A link corridor was then constructed between the old and the new buildings. This has now been demolished to make way for a new Day Hospice and all that remains of the pool is one wall which has been incorporated into the foundations of the new building.

Today, in the last decade of the 20th century, the exotic shrubs and trees so sedulously tended by Miss Fanny Hope and her gardeners have all gone, but Sir John McLeod's lawns still spread their greensward around the house and, although a set of Sir John Murray's fifty volumes of navigational charts were until recently within his former Edinburgh home as a reminder of the exciting days of the Challenger Expedition which gave its name to the house and unwittingly steered its course into the future, they are no longer there, but a complete copy of the mammoth Challenger Report is held by the National Library of Scotland in Edinburgh. Each one of the charitable organisations by which he has been succeeded has accepted the challenge of their own day and generation and, setting themselves faithfully and cheerfully to their tasks, have carried them, in the same pioneering spirit, nobly and honourably towards fulfilment.

(This chapter, down to this point and under the same title, has been produced as a booklet by St. Columba's Hospice.)

From 11th to 25th April 1992 the Fourth International Festival of Science and Technology was held in Edinburgh during the course of which several lectures were delivered on the subject of Marine science. One of these, by Dr Tony Rice of the Institute of Oceanographical Studies at Worthing, was largely devoted to the achievements of Sir John Murray. In the literature announcing these events the lecture given by Dr Rice was introduced thus, under the heading *Auld Reekie – the Early Days of Marine Science –*

At the turn of the century, Edinburgh was at the centre of the oceanographic world and the acknowledged leader was Sir John Murray, a Canadian-Scot, who made a fortune out of oceanography.

To deliver the lecture Dr Rice, dressed in the style of the period, assumed the character of John Murray and spoke as he might have done when looking back 'on the exciting developments in his own lifetime and forwards to the discoveries of our own day.'

Dr Rice was invited to pay a visit to Challenger Lodge and the site of Villa Medusa, and this he did, taking on, again, the character and dress of the 'intrepid mariner'. One of Edinburgh's less well remembered heroes, he and his work are still acclaimed by those who have followed him in the study of the ocean-depths – 'the last unexplored frontiers of the earth.'

CHAPTER 4

Trinity Mains Farmhouse and Woodbine Cottage

In York Road and at the edge of the cliff is Woodbine Cottage, shrinking away, as well it might, from public gaze, for this charming little early 19th century house, set within a garden which looks as if its design had not been altered since it was first laid out, has an intriguing reputation. It was a smugglers' cottage, says tradition, and moreover it had an underground passage which emerged at the foot of the cliff beside the sea. What it does in fact have is a concealed compartment beneath the floorboards, but as to the underground passageway, there is, to say the least, some room for doubt.

Myths and legends tend to gather around reputed features of this kind once the possibility of their existence has been suggested. This is well exemplified by Charles J. Smith in *Historic South Edinburgh* when writing about such a subterranean tunnel at Old Craig House. The last private occupant of that ancient dwelling was the renowned historian John Hill Burton who 'noted an underground passage leading from the thick-walled basement', and even he 'believed that this eventually emerged at Edinburgh Castle'. Actually, however, 'foundation excavations many years ago revealed that the tunnel, now largely blocked up, emerged only a short distance from the old mansionhouse, in the overgrown northern slope of the grounds.' Robert Louis Stevenson, as usual, got it right when he wrote, in *Edinburgh: Picturesque Notes*, 'these two words "subterranean passage" were in themselves an irresistible attraction, and seemed to bring us nearer in spirit to the heroes we loved and the black rascals we secretely aspired to imitate.'

If there is such a passageway at Woodbine Cottage it would have had to be blasted through solid rock, and negotiating it would have been an unenviable undertaking because of its steepness. But the history of the house can be explored, even if the secret tunnel cannot, although the question 'Was this a smugglers' cottage?' has unfortunately to be left unanswered too.

The story of Woodbine Cottage is linked to that of Hay Lodge (the former Trinity Mains Farmhouse of which it has hitherto been difficult to say exactly how much was incorporated into the later building) which, most interestingly in view of its later ownership, also contained a concealed hiding place. This consisted of a small apartment, in which it was possible for one person to hide in a crouched position, beneath the landing on a stair leading to the second floor of the house. It could only be closed by drawing a bolt on the inside which would not therefore be seen by anyone on the stair or on the landing. That smuggling took place in and around Newhaven is not in doubt, but whether one or both of these houses were involved in smuggling certainly is. The fact that they both came into the possession of one owner, however, encourages speculation.

On Ainslie's map of 1804 the landowner's name at Trinity Mains is given as 'Scott', but the Masters of Trinity House of Leith had started to sell off their lands on the Wardie Muir in 'parts and portions' (perhaps more because they found it profitable than because they wanted to get rid of farmland) shortly after the middle of the 18th century. Their farm therefore existed for approximately sixty years with ground being feued from it at various times before and after the accession of George III. The archives of Trinity House of Leith, held by the Scottish Record Office, contain no information concerning the sale of any part of Trinity Mains farm (and no plans of or information concerning the farmhouse), but from the

Register of Sasines at the Scottish Record Office it appears that Trinity House sold land to Alexander Smith, a baker in Edinburgh, under a few contract dated 26th December 1774, and that Alexander Smith was succeeded there by John Neall, a merchant in Edinburgh who later removed to Glasgow when he was followed at Trinity Mains by William Scott, Solicitor-at-Law. William Scott took possession, under a Disposition recorded on 14th April 1787 as well as by the usual 'delivery of Earth and Stone of the ground of the same', of the lands of Trinity Mains 'lying formerly within the Parish of St. Cuthberts or West Kirk but now by Annexation within the Parish of North Leith, Sheriffdom of Edinburgh.' This also entitled him to a seat in the West Kirk which went with the land. The Trinity Mains lands were bounded on the north by the High Road leading from Cramond to Newhaven and included the Welsh melon, the property feued (as early as the 1750s) by Trinity House to Pierre Lamotte, and 'the Orchyard with the ground upon which the farm houses of Trinity Mains and the offices thereof are situate', the 'whole ditches, dykes, hedges and planting' being included. The lands of Laverock Bank lay to the east. The High Road from Cramond to Newhaven was then the principal road in Trinity. It was also dangerous as parts of it were all too frequently swept away by the tidal Firth.

William Scott's son, Alexander Scott, W.S., who succeeded his father in ownership of Trinity Mains, was born in 1792. The name was also spelled 'Scot', e.g. in 1822/23 'Mrs Scot of Trinity' (William Scott having presumably died before this date), and 'Alexander Scot, W.S.' are both said to reside at '12 Heriot Row'. In 1825/26 'Alexander Scott, W.S.' was at '16 Northumberland Street, house Trinity'.

Alexander was appreciated to Joseph Cauvin, W.S., the eldest son of Louis Cauvin, Teacher of French in Edinburgh, an interesting character in the history of the city who taught that language to the poet Robert Burns and who founded Cauvin's Hospital (or school) at Duddingston. Alexander

Scott was married twice – first, in 1819, to Helen Sutherland Gardiner and second, in 1823, to Magdalene Blair. He died in Melbourne, in Australia, on 22nd May 1840 aged forty-eight.

In 1852 Trinity Mains House is recorded as being occupied by 'Jas. Robertson, accountant' and from 1853/4 to 1854/5 by 'James Mackay, gardener'. Then in 1855/56 the name changes to Hay Lodge. This new house was a rebuilding of, and included some part or parts of, the original farmhouse and was itself demolished in 1967. The two prominent Hay Lodge nameplates can still be seen attached to the low wall which replaced the much higher one and now apply to the Miller housing built on the site in the late 1960s. The question therefore arises: did Trinity Mains Farmhouse before its reconstruction have within it the trap door and secret chamber already mentioned which are known with certainty to have existed in Hay Lodge? That it was inserted in 1856 or later seems unlikely as conditions by that time (the arrival of the Chain Pier, the railway and an increasing population) had greatly reduced the need for such a feature whatever its original purpose – which had of necessity to be connected with a desire for secrecy – may have been.

The interior of Hay Lodge was of considerable interest and suggested its origins as a farmhouse rather than a 'grand residence'. Entrance (on the east side of the projecting wing) was into the west end of a long passage with a narrow 'boxed-in' (or 'walled-in') main stair, which had a hand-rail attached to the wall, from which a few steps led up to accommodation for a maid. A narrow secondary stair, that did not connect with the one below, rose between the first and second floors. At the east end a stable had been converted into a laundry but still contained the iron rings to which the horses had been tethered and had an outside water trough. At this end also were F. R. Graham-Yooll's 'cockfighting' room, which was next to the former stable, and an old larder. A puzzling anomaly was a second-floor room in the thick-walled gable at the west end to which no door or other access existed within the house but two windows of which (one of them in the gable) could be seen from the outside. One explanation for this mysterious apartment could be that, on the reconstruction of the house, it had proved impossible to include it in the new interior arrangements and it had consequently been abandoned and closed off; another that it was built like that at the beginning, and was possibly, even, never floored, although it does not appear to have been an attic; the latter explanation being the more likely. If such speculation is right, however, and the 'lost' room was indeed part of the original fabric, then it makes it highly likely that the secret chamber on the stair leading to the second floor was there too in its Trinity Mains Farmhouse incarnation. It also strengthens the likelihood that this was used, as suggested later, as a bolthole when the Press Gang were in pursuit of local seamen. The large single-storey projection at the front of the west end of the house was a later

Hay Lodge from the west. One of the two windows of the inaccessible room can be seen at the apex of the gable.

The entrance at Hay Lodge, showing the gablets and bargeboarding. The east wall of the projecting room is on the left. The three photographs, including that on the back cover showing the tower and the additional projecting room, are the only known views of Hay Lodge (*Photos by courtesy of Miss Perpetua Pope*).

addition and contained a sitting-room – very cold, especially in winter, as it was enclosed on three sides by outside walls which appear to have been of brick and harl construction. The dining-room was immediately behind it in the main building.

In the garden there were many trees, including damson trees, and peach and orchid houses as well as the old vinery, but in 1936 it was found to have been used during the Graham-Yooll occupation as something of a 'junk yard', although by no means all the strangely assorted items would be dismissed as junk in the 1990s. There were statues and figures looking out from the rampant greenery, and urns and old tramcar seats and even a small cannon (the cannon was later placed, as a gift, in the garden of Boswall House in Boswall Road), all of which and much more had to be cleared away before the garden could be put in order (and which revealed yet another facet of Fred Graham-Yooll's multifarious activities – the collecting (possibly buying and selling) of such artefacts of antiquarian or just quaint and random interest as he was able to acquire from time to time).

The retaining wall on East Trinity Road was of exceptional height (was this connected to the desire for secrecy and did it date from the Masters and Mariners' day – or perhaps from Alexander Scott's?) and had a door, as well, latterly, as double gates that led to a garage. A few years before World War II a cottage behind this wall was demolished, thus enabling the wall to be straightened (it was also lowered – and lowered much further when the modern flats were built) and the pavement widened. Was this perhaps the 'Trinity house cottage' in which the gardener James Mackay was living in 1854? Some ancient trees can still be seen, including the two tall firs at the extreme west end of the present Hay Lodge area. The free-standing tower (joined to the building when the garage was installed) had a room at the top commanding the famous north/south view, access being obtained by means of a spiral stair. As some decorative features on the projecting wing were repeated at the top of the tower it seems likely that both were built at the same time, and as these features appeared round the bargeboarded roof of the house as well this may be taken as fairly convincing evidence that these two additions date from the 1855 restructuring.

What then does all the available evidence add up to? Conceivably this:

(a)   that here was an early 18th century farmhouse which, with its rudimentary stairs and inaccessible room, was probably built, perhaps not unusually for farmhouses, without benefit of architect (hence the total lack of records, plans, etc.): one writer who mentions it says that, after its reconstruction, it 'was still a farmhouse'; this must mean that either it was still surrounded by a farm and occupied by a farmer, or that it still retained its farmhouse interior; the Post Office Directories rule out the former and the description of the interior during the period prior to its demolition would seem to confirm the latter:

and

(b)   that D. Clunie Gregor, who owned the house for so short a time and who changed the name to Hay Lodge, modernised the exterior, built out an extra room at groundfloor level and the statutory tower, and then sold it on at a profit – an early example of similar practice at the present day.

The evidence of the house having been adapted for the harbouring of seamen, or others, attempting to evade the attentions of the Press Gang has been *reasonably*, or *fairly*, well established, but the evidence of it having been adapted for the purposes of smuggling is not nearly so convincing. In medieval times stairs situated at opposite ends of a building were intended to impede attackers, but in the 18th century and near the coast they *could* have been intended to impede a customs officer. Most interesting of all in that connection, was there perhaps a secret entrance to the inaccessible room for the purposes of hiding contraband? The answer to that question, however, will never now be known.

All in all, it is difficult to avoid the conclusion that Hay Lodge *was* the Mariners' old farmhouse, the exterior of which had simply been 'Victorianised' (with gablets and bargeboarding) in exactly the same way as some Georgian houses were 'Baronialised' in the 19th century. And what of the sea captain and Mr Dulham? Impossible to prove, of course, but they just *might* have been the inventions of Frederick Richard Graham-Yooll!

Turning now to Woodbine Cottage, the plot of land on which it was later built was feued from Alexander Scott, W. S., of Trinity Mains in August 1818 by Alexander Wight, a banker, who was probably the banker of that name recorded at '12 Royal Exchange' (now the City Chambers) in the High Street. No private address is given. The cottage was built the following year and the land and house were sold back to Mrs Agnes Scott, 'widow of the late William Scott of Trinity', seven years later in 1825 for £550. Neither of Alexander's wives was called Agnes, but as this was the name of his father's widow it may be assumed that it was she who was the purchaser. The date of birth of Agnes Scott is not known but her year of death was 1861. Alexander, as we have seen, was born in 1792 and if Agnes was then aged, say, twenty, her year of birth would have been 1772. She would consequently have been eighty-nine or her death in 1861 when the house passed, under the terms of her Will, to her three grandchildren. They appear not to have wanted it and in 1865 it was sold for £450. The next (and to date the last) time it was sold was in 1936 when the price was £400!

Woodbine Cottage, the first house to be erected in what later became York Road (which did not become a made-up road until 1845) and probably intended as a week-end or summer retreat for Alexander Wight, contains two mysteries. One is the strange object resembling a long piece of tubular scaffolding beside the gate. It is planted in the ground, is attached to the wall by a large iron staple and rises to a considerable height. The most likely explanation is that this is a sewer-vent on a drain running under the property and was presumably put there when the house was built, although it is narrower than would be expected if this is indeed its function. A much larger and taller vent, very much like a Victorian lamp-post in appearance, was placed at the southern end of

Woodbine Cottage from York Road. The tall, narrow, tubular feature rising above the wall is probably a long-disused vent on an underground drain. (Other photographs of the house and garden are reproduced in *Further Traditions of Trinity and Leith*.)

York Road, probably when the rest of the houses had been built, and the Woodbine Cottage vent doubtless went out of commission at that time. The larger vent was only removed in 1994 and it seems a pity that it was not allowed to remain as a historic part of the townscape. The Woodbine Cottage vent has obviously, and fortunately, been forgotten! In a water-colour painting dated 1898 of the house on the corner of East Trinity and Laverockbank Roads formerly known as The Cottage, to which reference has already been made, a similar tall, tubular feature can be seen which once, no doubt, served the same purpose here.

The other (and greater) mystery at Woodbine Cottage is a room with a secret chamber beneath the floorboards and possibly, but improbably, an underground passage down to the sea. The chamber is about three feet square and has three steps, each one directly above the other, let into one side. In the middle of another side is what can only be described as a shelf-like projection which prevents the wall behind it from

90

being seen. It is not impossible that it was intended to conceal a means of access to an inner compartment above which the floorboards can *not* be lifted up. There would be no difficulty in stepping down into the chamber, but a foothold would be needed, or at least helpful, in getting out – and the explanation of the use to which it was put has to take account of these steps. If ill-gotten goods were placed inside the chamber this could be done from a kneeling position outside it, but if they were to be concealed in an inner hiding place it would be necessary to get into the outer chamber in order to put them there. As it is very obvious that these floorboards can be taken up, this lessens the likelihood of the chamber beneath them being the hiding place – which would also leave the steps without an explanation. But an inner compartment would not only explain the steps but make the discovery of the moveable floorboards (and it is very obvious that they can be so moved) much less of a disaster for the smuggler. So is there more beneath the floorboards than meets the eye? If so, then what is here is a well-thought-out place of concealment which may have been incorporated in the house when it was built. However, children have often played inside it and if there was anything more to be discovered it is likely that they would have found it!.

Why was Woodbine Cottage sold back to Trinity Mains? It is now clear, on the assumption that the hiding place in Hay Lodge was there in its Trinity Mains Farmhouse days as well, that from the year 1825 two houses with concealed compartments were in the possession of Alexander Scott (and/or his mother). Does this mean that he was the smuggler? Even if the Masters and Mariners did not practise these lawless activities, it could certainly not be claimed that the ordinary seamen were above indulging in them, and in any case the trading restrictions imposed upon its port by Edinburgh might well have provided an historic incentive for the Masters and Mariners as well! In the 18th and early 19th centuries Wardie Bay would have been quiet and remote and well suited for bringing small boats ashore during the hours of darkness. Those who 'go down to the sea in ships' are not normally noted for their interest in agriculture. Had they therefore, as well as their publicly declared desire to invest in land and to cultivate farm produce which could be sold to increase their revenues and provide charity in kind for the sick and aged among their members, an ulterior motive for creating a farm on the heights above Wardie Bay – and were the Scotts merely continuing a long-established 'tradition' at Trinity Mains? Trinity House, however, had disposed of its farm and farmhouse long before 1819 and so cannot be linked to the building of Woodbine Cottage in that year. Then, again, was Alexander Scott himself responsible for the Trinity Mains house hiding place? And did he deliberately get someone else to build a house with a somewhat similar feature and to sell it back – to his mother! – to avoid possible suspicion?

The particulars concerning Alexander Scott are taken from the *History of the Society of Writers to H. M. Signet to 1890* where he is called 'Alexander Scott, of Trinity'. His date of admission as a Writer to the Signet is given as 27th February 1817 when he was aged 25. Would he be likely to have been involved in smuggling at such a time, and why would he be prepared to put his professional status at risk by doing so? He was certainly living at Trinity Mains in 1825, the year in which Woodbine Cottage was sold back, so did he (and his mother) prior to that date let the old farmhouse to a 'professional' smuggler who obtained the run goods on their behalf? And did he himself instal the secret chamber in Woodbine Cottage which would remain a fairly isolated house at the cliff edge till York Road was made up in 1845?

Or, of course, is there some totally different explanation for these two puzzling features in these two houses? As Woodbine Cottage *was* such an isolated house in its early years, and as it was owned by a banker, it might be thought that Alexander Wight simply wanted a place of reasonable safety for valuables as the cottage could be seen as a tempting target for anyone intent on burglary (covered by a carpet, the removable floorboards might not be found by an intruder ignorant of their existence, although they would be by an experienced Customs and Excise official), but that is a less likely explanation for Hay Lodge where the bolt was on the inside of the secret compartment. Being just large enough to conceal a man (possibly two in a dire emergency), it is much more probable that the Hay Lodge hiding place, if, as seems likely, it was part of the original farmhouse, was used as a place of concealment from the Press Gang who were, after all, looking specifically for fishermen and sailors (though they took other people as well) to augment the depleted crews of naval vessels. The inhuman practice of impressment, which caused great suffering to the victims themselves, who had to endure the appalling conditions which prevailed on board the ships of the Royal Navy at that time, and to their families, was carried on for many years but was most widely used during the French Wars of 1793-1815, after which it was discontinued as a means of obtaining recruits.

This leaves the question of what sort of contraband might be hidden in Woodbine Cottage – and that immediately raises yet another problem. Tea, spirits and tobacco were the principal items smuggled, along with such varied goods as china, soap, playing cards and silk (and muslin and linen), but they were confiscated from the holds of ships which carried them in bulk containers such as ankers (1 anker = about 8 gallons) and hogsheads (about 50 gallons) which could hardly have been concealed in Woodbine Cottage. (It has however been suggested that brandy, for example, could have been hidden here after being transferred to bottles of the size currently in normal commercial use.) Tom McGowran, in *Newhaven-on-Forth, Port of Grace*, says that tea was the 'most profitable of the contrabands' and Campbell Irons in *Leith and its Antiquities* notes that 'when smuggling was a lucrative and comparatively safe practice, many devices were adopted to defeat the vigilance of the revenue officers, who were not, indeed, infrequently suspected of being in league with the smugglers. The vessels engaged in the contraband trade, which came as far up the Firth of Forth as Leith, rarely made two consecutive voyages without changing their appearance, so as not to be readily recognised by those who had reason to be suspicious of them on former visits. Very frequently, too, they would pass Leith, as if bound for Alloa or Bo'ness, and, after dark, would quietly drop down to the place where the cargo was intended to be run ashore.' In justice to the 'revenue officers', it has to be said that they often suffered severely at the hands of the smugglers, being physically assaulted, locked into the cabins of ships they had boarded or flung into the sea. The main smuggling period was the 18th century and the practice thereafter gradually declined. It did not die out, however, and indeed it is still taking place – though with rather different substances being smuggled!

There will probably never be an answer to the many questions raised but it looks as though Alexander Scott the lawyer, possibly in cahoots with Alexander Wight the banker, may have been behind whatever smuggling, if any, may have taken place, but this may of course be doing them both a gross injustice. All that can be said is that such evidence as there is could be taken to point in that direction.

Pointing in the opposite direction, however, is the fact that Boswall of Blackadder (of Wardie House) and Scott (unfortunately there are no entries for Boswall (more likely) or Scott (less likely) in the Dictionary of National Biography) contributed towards the building of the Chain Pier in 1821 and that they had plans for docks at 'Trinity Bay' (Wardie Bay) to be called Trinity Harbour. They also had capital of £250,000 – but it is fruitless to speculate as to where some of that might have come from!

In 1836 the Edinburgh Town Council opposed the right of Alexander Scott, who could not lay claim to shore rights, to erect a harbour north of his lands of Trinity. He wanted, says one account, 'to open up his grounds and connect them with

Edinburgh'. He had therefore enthusiastically pushed on the plan of running a railway to the Chain Pier and had been responsible for getting the project approved by Parliament. His impatience to get some return for all this work led to the railway company, of which he was a director, paying him £355 in consequence of which they were allowed to enter his property even before its valuation had been settled. Although the legislation had been passed in 1837 the Town Council of Edinburgh was bankrupt and the plans were shelved. Indeed it is understood that his impatience and frustration as a result of the difficulties encountered during his involvement in these developments were the reasons for Alexander Scott's emmigration to Australia. In 1842, two years after his death, an action was brought by the railway company against 'R. E. Scott, Esq., accountant and trustee of the late Alexander Scot's estate of Trinity'.

The Chain Pier possibly, but docks more certainly, would have brought smuggling to an end in the Trinity area. Or might they, on the other hand, if methods were changed and 'modernised', have facilitated it? The running of contraband had been a normal part of the fishermen's life, in Newhaven as elsewhere, and Leith was a notorious centre, having had a well-established fleet of smuggling luggers and yawls, and smuggled merchandise was brought in through Leith Docks on countless occasions. But the practice in Trinity would come to a natural end soon afterwards as the Victorian building programme got under way.

How many houses along the shores of the Firth of Forth contained evidence of smuggling or some other illegal activity? There is thought to be a secret passage behind a 'wall mural' in Caroline Park, a house in which political intrigue is believed to have taken place. It and Woodbine Cottage still survive, but the demolition of Hay Lodge which, as Trinity Mains Farmhouse, was the first building in what later became the clearly defined locality of Trinity, cannot be seen as anything other than regrettable.

On 1st April 1841, a year after the death of Alexander Scott, Dr James Browne died in Woodbine Cottage although his address at that time was No. 13 Comely Bank and the Woodbine Cottage title deeds do not mention him in the succession of owners. This information nevertheless would seem to be reliable as it was given by his son-in-law, James Grant. It is possible that his death was sudden and took place while on a visit to the house. Dr Browne's daughter Christine had married James Grant, the author of *Old and New Edinburgh*.

James Browne, LL.D. (1793–1841) was the son of a manufacturer in Coupar Angus and was born at Whitefield in Perthshire. His varied career started when he became a Church of Scotland minister although he decided initially to spend some time on the continent as tutor in a private family. Returning to Scotland, he took up a teaching position in Perth Academy and, simultaneously, undertook the duties of interim assistant to the minister of Kinnoul. It was about this

The two remaining fir trees in the centre still remain from the old Trinity Mains site in East Trinity Road. On the right are the flats which replaced the house and gardens of Hay Lodge.

time that he published, anonymously, a highly successful *History of the Inquisition* but, possibly because he saw little prospect of obtaining a parish, he abandoned the ministry and turned to the bar. An advocate by 1826, and having received the degree of LL.D. from St Andrews University, he nonetheless was unable to obtain a practice and made his final change of direction into the world of literature, editing the *Scots Magazine* for a short time and then becoming editor of *The Caledonian Mercury*. During his period as editor of this newspaper he fought a duel with Charles McLaren, the editor of *The Scotsman*, because of a dispute relating to a fine art criticism, but neither was injured in the encounter which took place near Ravelston at 7 a.m. on 12th November 1829. Later he was appointed assistant editor of the *Encyclopaedia Britannica* and was also the author of many published works. Towards the end of his life he converted to Roman Catholicism and, after his death at Woodbine Cottage, was buried in Duddingston Churchyard.

CHAPTER FIVE

Woodville, A Hidden House

Woodville is a hidden house in a concealed and quiet garden. When you take a summer walk down East Trinity Road the long, high wall to the left of the pavement will give no clue as to its existence behind the lawns and ancient trees that extend the garden far back from the street and public scrutiny. Nor will you fare better at the entrance gate in Laverockbank Road where the dark lime- and sycamore-lined avenue leads to the side of the house, the eastern wall emerging only gradually from the dark tree shadows, like the 'tunnel of green gloom' in Rubert Brooke's *Granchester*, as you approach it down the gravel path. But when you walk out onto the grass, in front of the classical garden urns at either side and the great circular rosebed (filled with crocuses in spring) in the centre, you are confronted by the beautiful and well-proportioned simplicity of a Georgian mansion in miniature which delights and surprises by its very unexpectedness.

The only ornamental feature of this most charming of Trinity villas is the doorway, with its white-astragalled fanlight and two sturdy flanking Tuscan columns. Even the rhones have been banished to the north and west sides so that nothing should detract from the plain regularity of the exterior which had, nevertheless, one very unusual characteristic undetectable from the front. The upper storey was confined to the south-facing frontage and was not continued above the rooms at the back. This trig little villa among the trees, so aptly named by those who built it, can, however, command one view more distant than a glimpse of flats to the south and some (incompatible) houses of more recent date to the imme-

The little Regency house of Woodville in its garden near the top of Laverockbank Road.

diate north, for the enduring mass of Arthur's Seat raises its extinct volcanic slopes just high enough to the south-east to be discernible.

1816 is a possible building date for Woodville which has all the appearance of a little Regency house, for it was on the first day of May in that year that the 'southmost half as divided and marked off by a thorn hedge of the lot or piece of ground in the West Park of Laverockbank' (on the level land at the top of the cliff) was sold to John Stewart who was thereby bound to pay a proportion of Minister's stipend and King's cess (tax) with other public and parochial burdens, the usual obligations undertaken on the acquisition of property. But as it was situated sufficiently close to the Forth he was also obliged to pay his share of defending 'the East, West and Middle Parks of Laverockbank' against encroachment by the sea. There was to be no manufactory or other operation carried on on the grounds or any work erected which might be a nuisance. When Kirkwood drew his map of Edinburgh in 1817 the name 'Mr Stewart' was printed across the area of which he had become proprietor, but it is quite possible that the house had been built a few years earlier, perhaps even as early as 1811, by the previous owner whose name of Anderson (Dick Douglas Anderson, probably the son of the Leith wine cooper Patrick Anderson who, as we have already seen, changed the name of the area from Larkbank to Laverockbank) can be read on maps predating that of Kirkwood. At all events, it harks back to the period at the end of the Napoleonic wars, a time when Martello towers had been erected round the coasts of Britain, including one at Leith, as fears of a French invasion ran high throughout the country. The avenue of trees which leads to the house has the reputation of having been planted to commemorate the famous victory of Waterloo in 1815.

For fifty-five years Woodville was the home of John Paris, a native of Bo'ness who, in 1924, purchased it from the family of W. M. Morgan, a commission agent and merchant with business premises at No. 3 Bernard Street. One of his two daughters, the painter Annie Morgan, had a studio at 58 Queen Street in 1910 and was President of the Scottish Society of Women Artists during the 1940s.

Vigorous and active to the end of a prolonged and ripe old age, John Paris pursued here the two great interests of a many-faceted career – gardening and chemistry. In his younger days he worked as a scientist with the Government Laboratory, travelled in Canada and Russia and held an appointment with the old Excise Department of the Inland Revenue. At Woodville he enlarged and recreated the garden, concentrating mainly on rhododendrons and many varieties of roses, although it was never without colour from early spring to autumn. Towards the end of his life the only assistance he would accept was with grass-cutting on the long, spreading lawn which stretched from a few feet in front of the house down to the beds of roses, delphiniums and dahlias at the other end. Two tall, branching deodars (*Cedrus Deodara* from the Himalayas, the 'divine tree' of the Indian poets) planted by him in the 1940s have matured among the older trees in this tree-sheltered garden, and he pointed out in particular a small-leafed weeping birch of a rare beauty and delicacy, the silver bark rising through the gently drooping branches. An attractive painting of this tree by W. Wight Pringle hung in one of the bedrooms and another by the same artist of the house itself was in the entrance hall. These more fragile trees contrast noticeably with the strong, dark foliage of the drive, a reminder that the sycamore is the old 'dool tree' of Scotland from whose boughs often hung the mortal remains of thieves and miscreants, while the lime was the tree ecclesiastical, creating, it has been said, a lofty 'Gothic' nave when planted in avenues.

In his ninety-seventh year, in May, the month of the rhododendron-flowering, John Paris conducted a party of seventy members of the Caladonian Horticultural Society around the garden, which covers three-quarters of an acre and was the scene of occasional summer fêtes and outdoor functions. In May 1972 it was the subject of an illustrated article in the magazine *Garden News*. Fortunate in its raised situation above the Firth, it is equally fortunate in being just too distant from the water to be adversely affected by the salt sea-spray.

John Paris liked to accompany the interested visitor into the house and up the curving staircase, with wrought-ironwork identical to similar stairs in the New Town which date from much the same period. He had brought with him to Trinity, he explained, the white-painted Dutch mantelpiece, probably about three hundred years old, and carved in high relief with flowers, shells and female figures, from an old house in Bo'ness, a house which had originally been the town's tolbooth and in which one of the last trials for witchcraft to be held in Scotland had taken place when six women and one man had been sentenced to death. The Bo'ness mantelpiece fitted to perfection round the fireplace in the principal Woodville bedroom.

In the drawing-room downstairs, to the left of the doorway, is an original mantelshelf, with shallower floral carving, inserted when the house was built. This room was furnished by John Paris with an admirable restraint which enabled each article of furniture, dating approximately from the late 18th or early 19th century, to be seen to advantage, including a Georgian writing desk, faded and polished into the mellow patina of old mahogany, and an oval table of the Adam era decorated with paterae and husks. The house contains two false doors, placed, to preserve the interior symmetry of drawing- and dining-rooms, in walls where insufficient thickness was available to provide for cupboard recesses and, opening the genuine six-panelled door in the deeper wall to the left of the drawing-room fireplace, he, or his housekeeper Miss Hunter, would reveal its treasures – the christening cup made at a Glasgow pottery with which the Paris family had for several generations been connected and hand-painted with flowers and the inscription 'John Paris born 13th January 1879'; a glazed earthenware water-bottle with the initials J P and the date 1791 cut into the glaze by the brother of Mr Paris's grandfather and, most interesting of all, an old snuff box found by his great-great-grandfather on the site at Bo'ness where one of Prince Charles's Highland Regiments had encamped on its way to link up with the Jacobite Army before the Battle of Prestonpans in 1745. On the other side of the hall is the dining-room, the only room in the house which, with dark-stained wainscoting and more sombre furnishings, retains the long-influential atmosphere of its Victorian years.

One alteration was made to the villa by John Paris and that

was the installation of a bathroom. This was achieved by creating a landing half-way up the staircase and projecting it, along with additional cupboards, out to the back, thus avoiding any interference with the building's appearance from the front and sides. It is quite surprising to discover that here was a house which in the 1920s was still without those facilities which by then were usually taken for granted in most well-maintained dwellinghouses. An old-fashioned bathtub, kept in a large closet later used as a china cupboard, was carried out, placed in front of the fire and filled with water from jugs and kettles.

Outside on the lawn are two ornamental summer-houses in

A Spring scene of Woodville house and garden.

the trees' shade, one of which was the tiny wooden 'laboratory' where John Paris conducted experiments in chemistry, and at the side of the house facing the evening sun was the greenhouse with its bright rows of plants and flowers.

The late Mrs Holroyd of Strathavon Lodge, Sir J. Y. Simpson's Firth-side retreat, had the unusual experience of delivering the Queen's telegram to John Paris on his 100th birthday in January 1979, when the weather during that severe winter was at its worst. Determined to get through the snow to Woodville, little more than a stone's throw away, if, as she herself put it, she had to crawl on her hands and knees, she went out just as the driver of the mail van drew up outside and asked her to direct him. (Due to the widely varying dates at which the Laverockbank Road houses had been built, their numbers are somewhat chaotic and misleading.) He had come too far, she said, and would be grateful, in view of the weather, if he would take her along with him in the van. On getting out at the gate he handed her the last delivery of mail for Woodville for the day. Miss Hunter greeted her at the door: 'Come in and see all the cards and flowers and telegrams – but there isn't one from the Palace'. 'Oh yes, there is', she replied, 'and I have been given the privilege of bringing it!'

John Paris died on 23rd November 1979, two months before his 101st birthday. He was related to the Burrell family of Glasgow, one member of which, Sir William, achieved lasting fame as the creator of the renowned Burrell Collection of works of art of international repute which had to wait many years before a suitable home could be found for their permanent display. Long-lived he may have been, but John Paris's life at Woodville was in part a sad and lonely one. It was to this house that he had brought his bride in the mid-1920s, not doubting that it would be the family home for many years to come, only to lose her and their stillborn child in the first few years of marriage. The garden, with its evocative 'oldness' and individuality which leaves a lasting impression on the visitor, became her memorial for over half a century.

Happily, Woodville is again in family ownership and further alterations, including the extension of the upper floor across the rest of the house to provide two further bedrooms and the building of a conservatory on the western side, have been made. But memories of the past, and of the recent past, still linger. Here in the fragrant quietness, as you sat taking tea with Mr Paris and Miss Hunter on the grass beside the rosebeds, the Victorian flats, briefly visible to the south when the green depth of foliage stirred and lifted, and the much more recent houses in Roseville Gardens on the level ground before the road plunges steeply towards the sea, seemed to fade strangely in the afternoon sun. Then, while the shadows lengthened in the dark lime avenue, a rustle of silk would become faintly audible above the rustle of leaves, and the long, high-waisted skirts of the Regency would come gliding towards you momentarily through the trees.

CHAPTER SIX

The Lands of Bangholm

Of the little hamlet of Bangholm not much remains. Bangholm House, which lay to the east of Clark Road, disappeared earlier this century. On a map of Edinburgh published in the 1920s an area approximately a quarter of a mile to the north of Ferry Road is designated 'Bangholm' and Bangholm Nursery is shown on both sides of the southern end of Clark Road. But the House of Bangholm Bower, consisting of a central block and two lower wings now approached from Bangholm Bower Avenue on the southern edge of Trinity still stands where it did. This is partly due to its having been absorbed, shortly before World War II, into the row of little villas then being built on the last stretch of ground belonging to the house to be disposed of, but even more to its having turned its back in silent resignation on the street, no doubt in nostalgia for its more spacious past, to face its Georgian entrance and white-astragalled fanlight towards a carefully tended little flower-garden bounded by a narrow rear lane.

The history of Bangholm Bower began when it was built as one of the 'principal mansions' in the area, as James Grant describes it, not far from the old road which led to Trinity 'between hedgerows and trees' before the roads to Granton and Queensferry were constructed. With its flanking pavilions and straightforward, symmetrical design, it is a typical example of the locally built early 19th century Trinity villa.

Gradually, over many years, the lands of Bangholm Bower have been sold off in large bits, small pieces and odd lots. The dismantling process can be traced in detail only after it had shrunk to one acre and thirty falls lying to the west and two roods, three falls and thirty-five ells bounded by the road from Leith westward on the south, the first title deed thereafter being dated 1802. In 1812 there was a disposition in favour of The Merchant Company of Edinburgh which, in turn, sold a large area of ground in 1872 to Mr Houston Mitchell. From him it passed to the Maxwell family a few years later with whom it remained for two generations. The second Maxwell widow, Mrs Miller Maxwell, disponed a half of Bangholm Bower next to the Caledonian Railway to the Town Council of Edinburgh together with a further 117 square yards at the corner of Ferry Road and (South) Trinity Road, the latter afterwards becoming the Scout Field in South Trinity Road.

The property was again sold in 1926 for £3000, and it was about this time that the house itself was altered and subdivided into three separate units, a central three-storeyed house flanked by two smaller ones in each of the wings with tree-planted gardens to the front and back. The remaining ground was feued for housing and the final street development, which put an end to Bangholm Bower's long life as a free-standing mainsionhouse, was completed shortly afterwards. The north side of the new street, called Bangholm Bower Avenue, spread bricks and mortar across the former rose garden, the site, if an old tradition can be relied upon, of the last duel to be fought in Edinburgh. Unfortunately the tradition does not include a date.

The large central house, while its street-numbered gate provides an uncompromising anonymity on the outside, preserves in the much-altered interior many interesting features from the past. The original back door has been elevated to front-entrance status and above it, lighting the curving wrought-iron staircase, is a tall, round-headed window in painted glass which is typical of others to be found in similar houses. There was considerable variety of design and this one, framed in an outer border of thistle, rose and shamrock motifs, contains four roundels, one above the other, depicting the seasons. In the circle at the top snowdrops represent Spring, while underneath Summer contributes roses and a lily, followed by ripened fruits for Autumn and finally a holly bush symbolising Winter is at the foot.

On the first floor the curtailed dimensions of the drawing-room retain, converted to electricity, four gas brackets projecting from the walls on adjustable brass scrolls, the pink glass globes dating from the time of the conversion. Adamesque plasterwork decorates the hall and staircase ceilings as well as friezes and cornices throughout the building. A white marble mantelpiece in the drawing-room contrasts with rose-pink fireplace tiles, also dating from the conversion, and another in one of the bedrooms, painted white, is decorated in the Adam manner with arabesque mouldings on either side of a jardinière containing grapes and vineleaves. A false door in the drawing-room once led to a still-room which is now part of the adjoining house in one of the wings.

Exploration uncovers a fascinating layout of narrow corridors which lead round, through other rooms and landings, to the original starting point. Liable to trip up the unwary, there is a sudden step down to a lower level where a modern kitchen and bathroom have been installed, and a narrow wooden door, which looks as though it gave access to a cupboard (another feature typical of its time and also to be found in New Town houses), opens on a secondary brass-railed staircase leading upwards, past a vast water cistern stretching far back behind the wood panelling, to the attic floor. Here, in the two large dormer-windowed attic bedrooms, the house hides one of its finest treasures, an incomparable view southwards to the Old Town skyline and (although this necessitates leaning out of the window) the Bass Rock and Berwick Law when visibility is good.

Since its sub-division the central house has had two unusual experiences. The first one occurred on the day of the Queen's wedding, an event which no doubt helped to impress it on the memory of the mother and daughter who had bought the

The original frontage, now the back, of Bangholm Bower,
a house that has shed its broad acres since it was built in the early
19th century.

house immediately after its conversion. (Miss Catherine
Thorburn, a descendant of the Logans of Restalrig, of whom
more later, died here, aged over ninety, in 1984.) In 1947
Edinburgh suffered an outbreak of 'weeping walls' due to rapid
fluctuations in the temperature throughout that summer. But
it was not water that was running down the staircase walls at
Bangholm Bower. It was what looked, to all appearances, like
blood! The cause of this alarming phenomenon was the rapid
condensation of the red paint (the famous red ochre so uni-
versally used in the 19th century) with which they had been
covered long ago and which had been overlaid with later, less
sinister-coloured, coats of paint.

109

No less disconcerting was the second dilemma – the discovery one morning of bulging ceiling plaster above the stair and the possibility of a cascade of water descending through the house. Water, however, was not the gremlin in the situation this time but, much more unexpectedly, air pressure, the pressure having built up against the plaster after an application of paint with an unsuitable chemical constituent, and the remedy was simple and permanent – its removal and replacement with distemper!

Today Bangholm Bower, having shed its acres gradually in roods and ells, and no longer sheltered and secluded by its ancient walls, stands in the contemplative dignity of age beside the neighbouring suburban villas, a few hundred yards from the Goldenacre crossroads and the Leith-bound traffic.

St. Serf's Church was built on part of the Farm of Bangholms, and the playing fields of George Heriot's School, across Ferry Road, were once fields belonging to the farm.

Originally a Chapel of Ease of St. Cuthbert's, St. Serf's roots lie in the mission work carried out by that church about 1899 when worship took place in an iron church. The name was chosen because St. Serf had been a contemporary of St. Cuthbert and the new church was in that part of St. Cuthbert's parish which was nearest to the Firth of Forth, St. Serf himself having founded churches throughout Fife. The building of a stone church began in 1902 and in October 1903 the wide nave with tall arcading and the south transept were opened for worship, the iron church (which had served the congregation for thirty years) being retained as a hall. It was given full status in 1912 with a parish disjoined from the parishes of St. Cuthbert's, St. Bernard's and Newhaven Churches.

Designed in a neo-Gothic style by the architect G. Mackie Watson, St. Serf's stands on the corner of Ferry Road, from which it is entered, and Clark Road. A spire and north transept were intended but never built, the gallery was opened in 1921 and in 1924 the chancel, vestry and session house were completed. The south transept was made into a chapel in 1972. An oak pulpit designed by the architect was donated, along with the font, by Mrs Currie of Trinity Cottage, the communion table being a gift from her family in 1921. The choir screen, with the figures of Christ between St. Andrew and St. Serf, was carved by C. d'O. Pilkington Jackson and installed in 1926. The Second World War delayed the building of church halls, but these were completed and opened, with an entrance in Clark Road, in 1960.

Finally, on Palm Sunday 1970, three two-light windows in the chancel depicting the *Te Deum* were dedicated, making a splendid addition to the spacious interior. They are beautiful examples of the work of Gordon Webster and replaced the original windows in that year.

CHAPTER SEVEN

Pilrig House

A country residence between Edinburgh and Leith was for many years of its existence an accurate description of Pilrig House. But towns no more than time are prone to standing still, and the City and the Port gradually but inexorably strode out towards each other across the intervening fields and ultimately met at Pilrig, a convenient point of junction trafficwise till well into the twentieth century. Its future dependent on enlightened conservation in an increasingly inimical environment, conservation lost out, and the house stood vandalised to an empty, gutted shell in a public park. Throughout a lifespan of almost three and a half centuries, a curious, colourful and continuous history can be traced between its rise and its ruin.

The name of Pilrig, originally Peelrig, is said to derive from an early peel tower which stood in the vicinity. In the sixteenth century these lands were in the hereditary possession of the family of Monypenny, lairds of Pilrig, one of whom, Robert, was killed on the battlefield of Pinkie in 1547 when that veteran intruder the Earl of Hertford, by then the Duke of Somerset and Protector of England, continued Henry VIII's attempts to destroy the Auld Alliance with the French and routed the ill-led Scottish Army beside the River Esk at Musselburgh. The Monypenny tenure came to an end in 1623 when Pilrig was acquired from them by Gilbert Kirkwood, a goldsmith, who built the house in 1638. For many years it remained a typical, sturdy, Scottish L-plan structure of the early seventeenth century in harled rubble and probably incorporated part of an earlier building on the same site. In

Pilrig House, built in 1638, and for long the home of the
Balfours of Pilrig, in a deteriorated condition in 1968 in Pilrig Park.

the roof above the attic floor were dormer windows ornamented with finials carved as crescents and fleurs-de-lys, two
bearing also the date of building. It being common practice at
this period to record, in addition to the date, the initials of
the founder and his wife on the walls where they first set up
house together, often in the attractive form of a 'marriage
lintel' above the door, one of the window pediments was thus
adorned at Pilrig when Gilbert Kirkwood married Margaret
Foulis of Ravelston and established himself in the domestic
style and comfort then available to a prosperous merchant and
his family. Several of the rooms contained wood panelling
which appears to be Memel pine, and this would certainly

113

have accorded with contemporary trading patterns across the North Sea, timber being imported from the Baltic in exchange for Scottish coal and salt. Tradition, however, asserts that it was cut down on the Burgh Muir, and that rough, virgin southern outskirt is known with certainty to have abounded in oaks which were used for the wooden projections of the 'timmer lands' that caused the narrow streets of the Old Town to become narrower by seven feet on either side. The influence of Dutch and Flemish architecture, so familiar to the Leith and other east-coast merchants who made the crossing frequently in the course of business, was reflected in the curving chimney gable in the centre of the south front, with a little circular attic window introduced as well. The classically columned doorway on this wall is probably of later date and was reached by a short flight of steps with an iron handrail.

The long association of Pilrig with the Balfour family began in 1718 when the property was bought by James Balfour, a merchant in Leith, who styled himself 'of Pilrig'. It was the fourth Balfour of Pilrig who, in 1828, made the extensive alterations to the house that gave it the external appearance which it retained for the rest of its active life, its latter years being devoted to such a variety of purposes as would have surprised, and eventually, when no further purposes could be contrived, greatly saddened its earlier owners. Balfour employed William Burn, an architect much in demand during the early nineteenth century and probably best known today for his detrimental 'over-restoration' of St. Giles, to fill in the angle of the 'L' in the original plan. This partially destroyed the older vernacular style, but besides increasing the accommodation it gave the Balfours, as they no doubt intended, a more modern and 'prestigious' mansionhouse.

Balfour Street, leading from Leith Walk down to the present Pilrig Park, was called after the proprietors of the estate and was originally an avenue of stately trees that 'opened westward from the Walk to the old Manor House' but was apparently never used as a means of access. The whins, heather and straw on the Pilrig policies, however, had proved more serviceable when, in remoter times, they were given by the lady of Pilrig House to be burned as a primitive disinfectant in the many unfortunate homes that were visited by the plague during outbreaks in the city, when all such dwellings were 'purgeit and cleansit with fire and water' before being re-occupied by those who had been spared its ravages. Like the Biblical lepers, these unclean victims were set apart on the Shore at Leith or the islands of the Forth, and their household effects, it being forbidden by law to wash them in standing water, were placed in the Leith River which it was hoped would carry their impurities like sewage out to sea.

In the last years of the seventeenth century an earlier James Balfour was caught up, along with many others fired with enthusiasm for that ill-omened venture, in the attempt to establish a trading colony in Panama known as the Darien Expedition. To this narrow isthmus of land lying between the Atlantic and Pacific Oceans, apparently so well situated for convenient commerce with the east and west, about four thousand Scotsmen set out in 1698 in search of an elusive fortune. Three ships left Leith on 26th July carrying the colonists. Disease, misfortune and the rivalry of English merchants doomed the enterprise from the beginning, and the sadder and wiser survivors who returned numbered not more than thirty. Several thousands who did not risk their lives but hazarded too much of their worldly wealth reaped a dire financial ruin from which most did not recover. James Balfour, a burgess and guild brother with his business in Leith, had lived in Milne's Court in the Lawnmarket and had had an interest in several commercial enterprises, including ownership of a shipbuilding yard in North Leith and partnership in a Leith soap works. He died, says John Russell, of a broken heart after the Darien misadventure, not realising that all, in fact, had not been lost. By the Treaty of Union of 1707 it was agreed that capital which had been invested in the expedition would be repaid with five per cent interest. These repayments were eventually, if gradually, made good, and James's eldest son, another James, was able to take advantage of this financial return to clear his father's debts and save some portion of his business. By 1719 all the Darien capital had been repaid, and by the previous year James Balfour had known that he was now a rich man. In John Russell's words, he bought forthwith the 'estate of Pilrig with its mansion and park, meadows and cornfields and silvery stream of Broughton Burn'. It was the same innovating James Balfour who obtained a monopoly in Scotland of the manufacture of gunpowder and sited his factory a short distance south-west of Pilrig near the Water of Leith. The area subsequently took its name from these activities, and the later manor house of Powderhall was long outlived by the robust old house of Pilrig.

A footnote was added to the history of the Darien disaster in 1979 when the wreck of the Leith ship the *Olive Branch*, previously known as the *Marion*, was discovered lying in thirty feet of water off Caledonia Bay, near Panama, during a two-year world circumnavigation called 'Operation Drake'. The fully loaded merchant vessel sank in 1700, when nearing the end of her voyage out to the Scottish settlement, when the ship's cooper went below, probably to help himself to some brandy, with a lighted candle which, igniting the spirits, set the *Olive Branch* on fire. Spearheads, cannon balls and Scottish coins were found when the wreck was investigated by divers.

James Balfour of Pilrig was one of the first commissioners to be appointed after the passing, in 1771, of the Act which marked the beginning of enlightened civic administration in Leith. The Act provided for the proper cleansing and lighting of the streets in South Leith, Yardsheads and St. Anthony's, as well as the supplying of fresh water to these areas.

It was in Pilrig House, still occupied by the same family, that the Rev. Lewis Balfour, maternal grandfather of Robert Louis Balfour Stevenson , was born in 1777, in later years becoming minister of Colinton Church. On its way towards

Pilrig and the sea at Leith, turning many a mill wheel as it went, the industrious little Water flowed, as it flows still, past the manse and garden so well remembered and described by R. L. S. himself. To his youthful imagination it had been, if not a torrent at the door, more excitingly a haunted stream beyond the garden. 'Down at the corner of the lawn,' he wrote, 'next the snuff-mill, there was a practicable passage through the evergreens, and a door in the wall, which let you out on a small patch of sand, left in the corner by the river. Just across, the woods rose like a wall into the sky; and their lowest branches trailed in the black waters.'

At Stevenson's death in 1894 the Balfour connection with the old family house at Pilrig had only forty-seven years to run. The first step towards its termination was taken in 1920 on the amalgamation of Edinburgh and Leith when, under the Extension Act of that year, the Town Council undertook to provide a public park in close proximity to the Port. Two years later, in fulfilment of this commitment, they acquired over twenty acres of the Pilrig estate, the bequest of the house on the death of the liferentrix, Miss Margaret Balfour-Melville, being part of the agreement. The conditions attached to this transaction are of considerable interest. The Corporation pledged themselves to the preservation of the building either as a museum or a charitable institution or to use it for some other purpose and never at any time to let it in apartments, divide it into tenements or allow it to fall into disrepair. Miss Balfour-Melville died in 1941 and the house and garden were taken over by the Council with some ceremony and public notice. Contemporary photographs show a well-preserved, lived-in mansionhouse with ivy growing across its walls. A sundial, bearing the words 'The path of the just is as a shining light', was placed at the front of the building on the west wall beneath the sloping roof. The dates 1718–1941 were also incorporated to commemorate the long period of ownership by the Balfours of Pilrig, whose tombs are in South Leith Churchyard.

In the years immediately following these changes the old house saw a diversity of occupants and occupations come and go. At different times it was adapted to meet the varying requirements of a Civil Defence centre, a boys' club and a firemen's hostel. In 1946 ten homeless families were given emergency accommodation in the twelve-roomed house, and by 1954 the Corporation let it be known that they could find no further use for it. It stood now without a reason for existence in a public playing field, and vandalism soon hastened its deterioration as doors and windows were broken and, as a consequence, bricked up. It was said that furniture had been piled behind the doors to prevent their being opened, but the contents did not remain inside much longer. Until 1969 the

The surviving shell of Pilrig House after the fire of 1971.

Pilrig House rebuilt as flats in 1986.

Corporation maintained a caretaker in solitary residence on an upper floor, but no repairs were ever carried out, and rainwater from the leaking roof put an end to its inhabitability.

For freely accessible, untenanted and decaying property the almost inevitable fate is fire, and in 1971 and again in the following year the inevitable happened. The roof and upper part of the house, where the most interesting architectural features were to be found, were destroyed completely, and the resultant ruin was then reduced in size and its remaining walls shored up for safety.

From time to time, both before and after this devastation, various suggestions were made by interested bodies to revitalise the building with a view to its resumption of some useful role in the community, but these were abandoned because of rising costs and other problems. To put flesh once more on the charred bones of Pilrig House was a daunting and expensive task, but a proposal to carry out external restoration and create six flats inside the shell of the 1638 building was at last agreed. The plan included the provision of sheltered housing

119

on adjoining ground and the sale of approximately 1.8 acres of Pilrig Park for residential development. Implemented with sensitivity, it has provided a happy alternative to the two hard options between which the house had been hovering for years – picturesque consolidation as a ruin, or demolition. The lairds of Pilrig, the terms of their bequest having been so soon forgotten, might conceivably have preferred the latter. Their descendants, however, gave the project the seal of their approval by their presence, on the 29th of November 1985, when, the original stones having as far as possible been reused and containing a stair of the old turnpike design, it was reopened as executive flats providing living space more in tune with the needs and aspirations of the 20th century.

CHAPTER EIGHT

Three Roads to Leith

By an odd historical coincidence, the origin of Leith Walk as the principal thoroughfare between Edinburgh and its Port can be attributed to the military strategy of an Englishman, none other than Oliver Cromwell himself, the only person ever to have deprived the country of a monarch. Angry at Scotland for proclaiming Charles II as its King and riding north to do battle with the Scots, he chose to threaten the capital by advancing towards it from the Port. In his *Traditions of Edinburgh* Robert Chambers describes what happened: 'At the approach of Cromwell to Edinburgh, immediately before the battle of Dunbar, Leslie, the Covenanting general, arranged the Scottish troops in a line, the right wing of which rested upon the Calton Hill, and the left upon Leith, being designed for the defence of these towns. A battery was erected at each extremity, and the line was itself defended by a trench and a mound, the latter composed of the earth dug from the former. Leslie himself took up his headquarters at Broughton, whence some of his despatches are dated. When the war was shifted to another quarter, this mound became a footway between the two towns'. Cromwell having been thwarted on Leith Walk (though not at Dunbar), the way was now clear for Charles, who regally rode along it from the Kirkgate into Edinburgh after being crowned at Scone.

During the following century, in 1748, Leith Walk, or Leith Loan as it was called originally, was described as a 'handsome gravel walk, twenty feet broad, which is kept in good repair at the public charge, and no horses suffered to come upon it'. In the course of time a second footpath was made at the bottom of the rampart, eighteen feet below the one on top, and to avoid confusion they were known as the High Walk and the Low Walk. A surviving example of the latter can still be seen at Springfield Cottage which stands at the foot of a flight of steps. A wooden paling prevents unwary walkers from falling down to the lower level. The street was left in this pedestrianised condition until 1769 when the new North Bridge was built to link the Old Town of Edinburgh with the open fields to the north upon which Princes Street and the New Town were eventually to spread out. As there was considerable opposition to this extension of the city boundaries, however, it was deemed advisable to suppress this information, and it was publicly announced that the new bridge was intended to facilitate communication between the City and the Port.

As a result of this new level access, the journey to Leith could now be made conveniently by horse and carriage, and the gravel surface of the Walk was soon churned into dust and pounded into pot-holes by the wheels and horses' hooves. This situation was tolerated, surprisingly, till the beginning of the nineteenth century when a 'splendid causeway was formed at a great expense by the city of Edinburgh, and a toll erected for its payment'.

Chambers recalls the Gallow Lee, a grim reminder of those bygone days when the country administered a stern public justice as rough, in many cases, as its unkept roads. 'One terrible peculiarity attended Leith Walk in its former condition. It was overhung by a gibbet, from which were suspended all culprits whose bodies at condemnation were sentenced to be hung in chains.' The ground on which it stood, adjacent to Shrub Hill, contained large quantities of sand, and the soil, enriched with the bones of centuries of malefactors, was sold by a speculating proprietor to be converted into mortar for the New Town houses!

Leith Walk in the early nineteenth century was a scene of 'enjoyment peculiarly devoted to children', and 'even the half-penniless boy might here get his appetite for wonders' gratified. In addition to caravan-shows, street singers and organ-grinders, few who had seen it as children ever forgot the waxworks 'which occupied a laigh shop opposite to the present Haddington Place'. The doorway of this entertaining establishment was decorated with parrots and birds of Paradise and a diminutive wax gentleman in the outmoded dress of a French courtier of the previous century who sat 'reading one eternal copy of the *Edinburgh Advertiser*'.

Leith Walk is described in an Edinburgh guidebook of about 1919 as having, some fifty or sixty years previously, been 'bounded on each side by nurseries, but [it] is now one continuous line of houses and shops, so that there is now no actual division between the two towns', the junction being at Pilrig.

It was in Leith Walk, in June 1821, that Thomas Carlyle, then living in Moray Street (subsequently Spey Street) near Pilrig, experienced the 'sudden spiritual awakening' which he afterwards transferred to his philosophic Germanic hero in *Sartor Resartus*. Carlyle re-enacts in the Rue St. Thomas de l'Enfer in Paris the salutary change in his attitude to life which he himself had met with in Leith Walk. He remembered the very spot where it occurred, 'just below Pilrig Street', as Professor Masson has recorded in his essay on Carlyle's Edinburgh life, while 'on his way to Leith'. As this incident happened immediately after his first meeting with Jane Welsh, whom he later married, the two events are probably not unconnected!

In the later nineteenth century Leith Walk seems to have become a sadly neglected thoroughfare. In a *cri de coeur* to the *Leith Burghs Pilot* in 1866, a correspondent complains of a lack of conveniences of more kinds than one, including drinking fountains and seats on which to 'rest and be thankful'. He deplores the unrepaired condition of the street which in wet weather 'represents a series of miniature fish ponds' and would 'disgrace a third class fishing village'. The Town Council, he says cynically, should 'mend their ways' in the 'Leith division of the Walk'.

Street names in this area often commemorate people who lived or had their business premises there. Thus the quaint, curving little side street known as Stead's Place recalls Mr Stead and his card factory (which made combs for carding wool), and at the end of Smith's Place, facing the Walk, the elegant and classical but now commercialised mansion called Smith's Place, built in 1812, has ensured that its owner's name would be given to the street. Behind the Walk on the other side, at Shrub Place, survives the Georgian country house of Middlefield (no doubt so named in reference to its

Middlefield, a Georgian country house surviving behind Leith Walk.

original surroundings), the straight-line of the street going along in front of it. Built in 1796, this attractive building, with a pilastered doorway beneath a pedimented central window flanked by two Gothic-glazed Venetian windows, and crowned with a gabled attic storey, deserves to be made more of and restored. Mr Anderson's Iron Foundry was on the other side of his garden wall and, with the exception of a few houses on the east side at the foot of the wide thoroughfare to Leith, the ground here was mainly open and undeveloped.

Before the completion of Leith Walk the two principal routes to Leith were Bonnington Road on the west and, as its name implies, Easter Road from the opposite direction. The area around the London Road end of the latter has been connected with the name of Norton since the second half of the eighteenth century, the association beginning when the Hon. Fletcher Norton, son of Lord Grantley of Yorkshire and Attorney General in England, came to Scotland after the unsuccessful Jacobite Rebellion of 1745. He was appointed a Baron of the Scottish Exchequer in 1776 and took up residence in a house, long since demolished, which stood on the site of Abbeyhill Station. Winning the confidence and respect of the people as a Judge, he soon overcame the prejudice and suspicion which still prevailed against the English. With his Scottish wife and family, he lived at Abbeyhill until his death in 1820, and his name is still commemorated in Norton Place and in a single surviving dwellinghouse now curiously situated in a drying green behind Easter Road. This is Norton Villa and, although still, happily, occupied as a family home, it is completely screened from view by the shops and tenements of one of the busiest streets in the district. Bay windows on both floors on one side, and a barge-boarded porch outside the entrance in the centre, give a Victorian appearance to this little, reputedly eighteenth-century, building.

Bonnington Road has witnessed the thriving life of its village by the Water of Leith where the earliest woollen manufacturers in Scotland lived and traded, and, when the *Great*

Michael was launched in 1511, James IV, grandfather of Mary
Queen of Scots, rode across its bridge in a Royal progress to
that other port of Newhaven which he had vainly hoped
would outstrip Leith in nautical pre-eminence. Today the road
will lead you past the remnants of the old Bonnington (or
Bonnytoun) Village without even hinting at its presence, but
opposite the Bonnington Road side of Rosebank Cemetery,
opened on the corner of Bonnington Road and Pilrig Street
in 1846, the modernised and repopulated village, with access
from Newhaven Road, is still there although it has lost almost
all its character – in spite of a mill-wheel set up to remind it

Bonnington Village, before its re-orientation to the 20th century
behind Newhaven Road.

of its past. For years the truncated limbs of the old viaduct that used to carry the little branch railway line that ran nois-ily above the crossroads at Bonnington Toll (and had been cut off at this point) rose, sullen and foreshortened, behind the village like an unpropitious signpost to the future. Backing on to Newhaven Road were the disused and disconsolate mill and granary buildings with the gaunt and empty Mill House adjoining at right angles, a makeshift outside stair indicating that it had once been subdivided to house two families. Although the site had been occupied by mills since the 15th century, the granary dated from the 18th and the mill itself

Bonnington Mill, long disused and now demolished.

127

(which was closed in 1967) only from the 19th. In the late 1970s permission was obtained by a firm of building contractors to create modern residential accommodation within some of the village buildings which it had been agreed should be retained. It is highly unfortunate, however, that by the device of waiting for three years and then resubmitting similar plans for the demolition of the mill and granary to those which had been initially rejected, they were allowed, in 1982, to carry this out for the purpose of making an entrance from Newhaven Road when another already existed in Bonnington Road. Only part of the facade of the Mill House, which had

Bonnington Mill House, shortly before demolition. All that remains is the central façade incorporated into new housing.

been in a badly deteriorated state, still remains incorporated into the walls of the new houses on either side.

Beyond, and nearer the Water of Leith from which a lade once bore its waterpower to turn the mill-wheel, are a row of restored cottages and the old mansion of Bonnyhaugh. A three-storeyed, rubble-built house, it was erected in 1621 by the Town Council of Edinburgh, who had purchased the mills four years previously, for a Dutch dyer called Jeromias van der Heill whom they had brought over from Holland to teach the craft in the city. About 1713 it became the 'secluded villa' of Bishop Robert Keith, scholar, historian and churchman. His *Catalogue of Scottish Bishops* was a valuable work of

The House of Bonnyhaugh, the home of Bishop Keith at the time of the Jacobite Risings, before conversion into flats.

reference of the Scottish Episcopal Church, and the list of subscribers to his *History of the Church and State of Scotland* read, says Chambers, like a 'muster roll of the whole Jacobite nobility'. Bishop Keith corresponded with Prince Charles Edward Stuart in France, but on the subject of ecclesiastical rather than political affairs. Having ministered conscientiously to his small Episcopal flock for many years, he died in Bonnyhaugh in 1757 and was buried, deeply mourned by them, in the Canongate Churchyard. The Bonnyhaugh interior was redesigned to provide a dwellinghouse and two flats. The adjoining smithy is now a house and the entrances to both it and Bonnyhaugh have been moved to the back of the buildings, the latter being approached by means of reproduction forestairs.

From Bonnington Toll down to the site of the old mill, Newhaven Road was bounded by the garden wall of the strange little mansion of Stewartfield – a high structure with a massive chimney stack crowning its steeply pitched roof – the casting down of which has to be laid at the door of a previous generation. In recent years the site has become the industrial estate of Stewartfield, the Powderhall Bronze Foundry being one of the businesses situated here.

In the mid-19th century, however, very different activities were taking place in the grounds around the house. A newspaper advertisement of 1840 reveals all:

STEWARTFIELD
BONNINGTON TOLL
Grand Eruption of the
BURNING MOUNTAIN VESUVIUS
WITH ADDITIONAL EFFECTS.
This evening, Saturday, August 29th, THE
GARDENS will be brilliantly illuminated
with thousands of Variegated Lamps, and
adorned with the statues of Ceres, Flying
Mercury, Flora, Cupid and Psyche.
NEAPOLITAN FONT

Antique Pillar from the Temple of Thebes,
BACCHUS and ARIADNE
Cast by J. Thomas.
By permission of Lieut.-Col. the Hon C.A.
Wrottesley, commanding the 29th, the excellent
and efficient BAND of the Regiment will be
in attendance.
Admittance One Shilling.
Doors open at Six – Eruption to commence at Nine.
ERUPTIONS ON MONDAY, WEDNESDAY and SATURDAY.

Undoubtedly a 'spectacular' it would be hard, and expensive, to emulate today when the admission charge would have to be rather more than the original one shilling (5p)!

Still standing in Ferry Road, but architecturally different from the rest of it, is Bonnington Bank House with its little forecourt garden and larger one behind. It is adjoined by the lower addition which served for a number of years as the Coach House Theatre and has recently been demolished and rebuilt. This late Georgian building with Victorian extensions was the town house of the Earls of Mar and Kellie and was later used by the Roman Catholic Church as a Laity Centre. After extensive renovation and refurbishment, and with an extension added to the east wing, it reopened as the Bonnington Nursing Home in 1990.

In Ferry Road Bonnington Bank House was the French Consulate for Leith and Agra Lodge, now subdivided, the German Consulate for Leith in the 1920s, while the present Victoria Park Hotel was built in 1859 (see *The Lands of Warriston* by Mrs Z. Ashford in the *Book of the Old Edinburgh Club* New Series Vol. 3 (1994) as Chancelot Villa.

These highways of ancient origin are still the roads that lead to Leith, but they can now be traversed with greater rapidity than could be achieved by those who were carried thither by the stage coach around two hundred years ago; it 'took an hour and a half to go from the Tron Church to the Shore', and was 'a great lumbering affair on four wheels, the two fore painted yellow, the two hind red, having formerly belonged to different vehicles', and was drawn by a pair of 'ill-conditioned, ill-sized hacks'. At the end of the 20th century the traffic faces other and acuter problems, change follows frequent change upon the face of Leith, and few people would now recognise either an old description of the Walk, that former rampart of defence against the invading Roundheads (whose battle on the site of Leith Links with its defenders was re-enacted in 1983 by the Sealed Knot Society as part of the 500th anniversary celebrations of South Leith Church), or the gastronomic rewards which awaited its perambulators. It was, wrote John Geddie, 'the favourite "walk" of citizens, old and young, on their way to enjoy the fresh salt breezes on Leith pier and to put an edge on appetites that could afterwards be blunted by feasting on the succulent "Pandore oysters", for which the Old Ship Inn and other taverns on the Shore were famed.'

CHAPTER NINE

North Leith

North Leith (of which Trinity later became a part) and South Leith began life as completely separate communities and remained so until comparatively recent times. The latter was in the hands and at the disposal of the Lairds of Restalrig, then both a larger and a more important place than the embryonic port, and the former belonged to the Abbey of Holyrood. Having therefore been in the parish of 'Holyrood House and Canongate', it did not become the parish of North Leith until 1606. Because of this, and in reference to the name of the Abbey, North Leith – the area benorth the brig – was known as the 'Rude Side' (rude or rood meaning cross). One of its enjoinments was to provide fish for the Abbot and canons whose abstention from meat on their frequent fast days was obligatory, and rents, as elsewhere, were then often paid in kind. In the late 15th century Abbot Robert Ballantyne built a bridge of 'three stonern arches' over the Water of Leith, and the street that led from it was the main thoroughfare in North Leith until the provision of a drawbridge at Tolbooth Wynd in 1788 created a new and better one in Bridge Street. As it was a hindrance to shipbuilding, much of which took place on the north side of the river where the first docks were sited, the old triple-arched crossing was then demolished. (In *The Port of Leith: its History and its People* the author, Sue Mowat, points out that, although the date of the first bridge is usually given as 1493, this bridge is in fact mentioned in a charter over fifty years earlier.)

The church of St. Ninian was also built by Abbot Ballantyne at the end of the bridge to spare the inhabitants the long and arduous walk to the Abbey church where they had worshipped until then. St. Ninian's, with its distinctive latticed wooden steeple, later became the parish church of North Leith, and the remains of the building, best seen across the river from The Shore, are still a conspicuous feature in the Leith townscape. It was not replaced as the parish church until 1813.

When the new Georgian North Leith Church, designed by William Burn, was built in Madeira Street in that year, its graceful spire rose from the surrounding fields as it rises now above the well worn streets and buildings of its present environment. A much older foundation, however, was the Hospital, with its chapel and burying ground, of St. Nicholas which disappeared in the mid-17th century when Cromwell's Citadel obliterated all else on the ancient site. North Leith had laid its citizens to rest in St. Nicholas churchyard, and to compensate for its loss the city gave them 'a garden extending to the river bank' in Coburg Street, to quote John Russell, which served as the only cemetery until the opening of Warriston in 1843 and Rosebank (in the grounds of the demolished Rosebank House which had been the residence of Lord Reay in the 1760s) three years later. Robert Nicoll, known as the Keats of Scottish poets as he died in his early twenties, is buried in the Coburg Street ground, and near the gate is the altar-tomb of Thomas Gladstone (grandfather of the Victorian statesman) who was an elder in North Leith Church.

At the top of Bonar Place, off Ferry Road, is the entrance to Letham Park. Originally known as Chancelot Park, it was bought in 1936 by A. J. Letham of the Boys' Brigade who gave it, after having it suitably laid out, to the Leith Battalion for their athletic activities. For twenty-four years he was captain of the 1st Leith Company, connected to North Leith Parish Church, and in March 1930 had been presented with a testimonial to mark his period of service. A metal plaque at the gate is inscribed, 'To the memory of Alexander John Letham and in grateful appreciation of his generosity and service.

Erected by The Leith Battalion, The Boys' Brigade, 28th April 1951.' Another park, called Keddie Gardens, is further along Ferry Road at Largo Place and has steps down to the Water of Leith on the left-hand side.

Cromwell's Citadel was erected on the beach with the salt spray flung against its walls in rough weather, but the sea has gradually been banished further away. This fortification was granted by Charles II to the Earl of Lauderdale who called the complex of buildings, in the monarch's honour, Charlestown. But the earl soon disposed of it to – predictably – the city of Edinburgh, and the houses it contained were then let out. Various commercial ventures were set up within it, including a glassworks, and it had a history of different uses and adaptations until its final demolition. The arched pend of the principal entrance on the east side is all that survives to the present day. Beside it, and built in Dock Street on part of the Citadel site in 1839, is the former Mariners' Church, its two octagonal towers no longer supporting spires and its interior converted into offices.

After the Reformation in 1560 the ecclesiastical overlordship in North Leith was superseded (together with St. Leonards and most of the village of Broughton) by the secular superiority of the Earl of Roxburgh. Canongate was also in the earl's possession, and he sold it, along with North Leith, to the Governors of George Heriot's Hospital, from whom the latter passed in 1639 to the Town Council and Magistrates of the City of Edinburgh.

In 1780 a ship called the *Fury* was built in North Leith for the British Navy, and it was at that spot, in 1812, that the Custom House was constructed in the prevailing Greek style to the designs of Robert Reid, one of the architects of the Second New Town of Edinburgh and the last of the King's Architects in Scotland. Prior to its rebuilding here in Commercial Street it had been situated, in very inferior premises, in Tolbooth Wynd.

Also on the Rude Side is all that remains of Leith Fort, two guardhouses built in the Georgian style at the end of the 18th century after the legendary John Paul Jones had come close, had he not been frustrated by the gale-force winds, to breaching the all-too-inadequate sea defences of the port. A large housing complex now covers the site of the main Fort buildings.

The new Town Hall (now the Leith Theatre) and, in front of it, the Public Library were built, at the eastern end of Ferry Road, during the years 1929–32 and occupy the site of the old North Leith Manse. The manse had been built about the year 1800 and by 1924 had become difficult and expensive to maintain and was sold with permission for its demolition and the erection of a public hall for Leith.

Round the corner in North Junction Street the former Scandanavian Lutheran Church fulfils a new and useful function not just for Leith but for the whole of Edinburgh. Its Scandinavian-style steeple rising on the northern side, this little building, says James Scott Marshall in *The Life and Times of Leith*, 'remains as a memorial to the days when Leith's trade with the Baltic countries created a large floating population of Scandinavian sailors in the Port'. In 1988, abandoning its association with the sea, it became the Leith School of Art founded by Mark and Charlotte Cheverton as an innovative teaching project, for beginners as well as for the more experienced, including drawing, painting, sculpture on a small scale, and printmaking within its programme of day and evening classes. Their work was a deliberately Christian-based initiative, so the oldest Norwegian Lutheran seamen's church outside Norway did not abandon its original *raison d'être* along with its maritime connections.

After acting as a travelling secretary for art colleges with the Universities and Colleges Christian Fellowship, Mark was appointed head of the Art Department at the Edinburgh Academy. Later, when he and Charlotte, a painter, teacher and art therapist, had married, Mark gave up his secure employment with the Academy and they set about finding suitable premises for their joint venture. A limited company with charitable status was then formed. On completion of the necessary alterations, the Norwegian Church quickly justified their choice of building in which to dedicate themselves to their vocation, and they were greatly helped by substantial gifts of money. Here was faith in action, with teaching and art therapy combining to meet the varied needs of handicapped children, adults seeking release from occupational stress and tension and people who just wanted to learn or to improve their capabilities.

But hard on the heels of their success came tragedy. Mark and Charlotte Cheverton were killed in a road accident in September 1991. A commemorative exhibition of their art and teaching, which included the work of some of their students, called *Freedom within a Framework* was held in the Leith School of Art the following year: but their best memorial is the school itself and the fact that their work in the old church goes on, work which, but for the determined efforts of two inspired and dedicated founders, would never have become an achieved reality.

'It was only in Victorian times that North Leith lost its rural aspect', writes James Scott Marshall, Newhaven as well as Trinity being incorporated in it, and it acquired its own railway station, a Greek-style building still to be seen, although no longer used for its original purpose, at the corner of Commercial and Citadel Streets, in 1846. Separated only by the Water of Leith, different traditions nevertheless grew up and were perpetuated in each section of the port. John Russell mentions one of them. 'For long after the Reformation North Leith rang its bell at 10 p.m., while South Leith sent round the town drum at the same hour to warn all people within doors. "Elders' hours" had to be observed in old-time Leith.'

CHAPTER TEN

The Port and The Crown

'The cannon-shots from the galleys, as they contrived to near Leith Harbour, were, doubtless, a sufficient advertisement. Soon, so far as the fog would permit, all Leith was in proper bustle, and all the political and civic dignitaries that chanced to be in Edinburgh were streaming to Leith.' Thus did David Masson, Professor of English Literature at the University of Edinburgh at the end of the 19th century, describe, three hundred years after the event, the arrival in Scotland of Mary, Queen of Scots, after thirteen years at the French court, to enter fully and inexorably into her inheritance of a crown, an ancestral palace and a turbulent and troubled country. The day, wrote John Knox, who might be expected to remember it, was so dark and 'the myst so thick' that 'skairse mycht any man espy ane other the length of two pair of butts'. Mary had set sail from Calais on 14th August 1561, two French galleys and other ships conveying the Queen, representatives of the French nobility and their 'rich and splendid baggage' towards the fog-bound Scottish coast.

When she stepped ashore 'she took some rest', says Professor Masson, 'in the house in Leith deemed most suitable for her reception, the owner being Andrew Lamb, a wealthy Leith merchant'. The house, undoubtedly rebuilt but most likely standing on the same site, is well known as Lamb's House at the present time. It is probable that Mary often looked back to that day of mirk and mist, so typical of her capital and its seaport but also so prophetic of the clouds that were soon to cast their shade on her uneasy reign. She was not the first of Scotland's queens to land at Leith, or to have had cause to

Lamb's House, once a merchant's quayside residence, and now one of the best-known buildings in Leith, where it serves as an old people's day centre.

lament 'the surfett weat and corruption of the air', as Knox so tellingly expressed it. Her father, James V, before his second marriage to Mary of Guise, the mother of the Queen of Scots who succeeded to the throne when just a few days old, had wedded the beautiful but delicate Magdalene, daughter of Francis I of France, who died – the 'weat and corruption of the air' being too much for her to thole – only eight weeks after stooping down to kiss the soil of Scotland at disembarkation in her husband's kingdom.

To the earlier Mary, daughter of the Duke of Guise, Leith was to become much more than a landing stage *en route* to

Edinburgh Castle. It was her misfortune, wrote Chambers in the *Traditions of Edinburgh*, 'to be placed in a position to resist the Reformation. Her own character deserved that she should have stood in a more aggreable relation to what Scotland now venerates, for she was mild and just, and sincerely anxious for the welfare of her adopted country'. Like her daughter, she would not abandon the ancient faith of France, and her last outpost before defeat was the Port of Leith. Though by then the Queen Regent was ill and, indeed, dying, she defended it well with strong support from the French who in June 1548, under the Scottish flag, sailed into the roads of Leith in twenty-two galleys and six hundred other ships, as recorded by Calderwood. The besieged were frequently the attackers in this bitter struggle, and the English army, which reinforced the 'raw levies' of the Lords of the Congregation, won no quick or even outright victory against Mary and the French who made several sallies outside their own fortifications when battle between the opposing sides was joined with 'sword and pike' on the Links of Leith.

Little evidence of these old wars is left today, except on the Links themselves where the English raised two mounds, armed with guns, 250 yards apart. Cannon were also placed on the tower of St. Anthony's Preceptory which has vanished from the scene as well. The townspeople of the port were not slow to change the martial nature of the mounds which were eventually taken over as convenient playgrounds by their children who, finding it a steeper climb, called the larger of them Giant's Brae. Lady Fife's Brae was their name for the other after the Countess of Fife who lived immediately southwards of the mound in Hermitage House. Cannonballs fired into the 'Kirk of Leith' on 15th April 1560 are preserved inside the entrance to South Leith Church. Writing in the 1880s, Grant adds a pleasant, peaceful footnote to the history of these mounds. 'When the young grass is sprouting in Spring', he writes, 'the zig-zags that led therefrom to the walls can often be distinctly traced in the Links'. Much larger military structures than the mounds were Pelham's Fort at Restalrig and Mount Somerset in the Broughton area called after the English officers in charge of them.

But Mary of Guise did not live to see the end. She considered the possibility of her return to France and the appointment of a new French Regent in her place; she even attempted to sue for peace with England; but on 10th June 1560, the year that saw the establishment of the Reformed Church in Scotland, she died, while waiting anxiously for news from Leith, in Edinburgh Castle.

Her daughter, widowed by the death of her French husband (they had been briefly King and Queen of France and Mary (aged 18) was now the Queen Dowager), condemned herself to certain sorrow when she married her cousin Henry Stewart, Lord Darnley, and it is pleasant to read of a charitable measure enacted jointly during their short married life. Having been petitioned to do so, they granted power to the skippers of Leith, for the better ordering of navigation, to 'take tryall' of all seamen and apprentices before allowing them to sail, and to apply the fees, and the fines imposed on those found wanting, to support the poor.

In 1568, when Mary left Scotland for the last time, she did not go from Leith, but by the Solway Firth and in a hurry and without a crown.

If the seagate to Edinburgh meant entrances to dool and skaith to his mother and grandmother, James VI took with him happier memories of the Port to his English inheritance when he added that other and much more coveted crown of the southern kingdom to his regalia. It was from here that he set out, in October 1589, to claim Anne of Denmark, who had been frustrated by westerly gales in her journey towards Scotland, as his bride. More fearless in the face of potential danger than he often showed himself, James braved the hazards of the waning year and sailed, like the saintly Brandan, to the northern main. The marriage ceremony, performed by The Rev. David Lindsay of South Leith Church, took place in

Norway, where Anne was stormbound, almost as soon as he set foot on land.

The king and queen then spent some months in Denmark before the sea-journey back to Leith in the April or early May of 1590. James, who would not return to Scotland without a Scottish pilot ship, had sent off a message to the Provost and Town Council of Edinburgh requiring them to find and furnish one to fetch him home. They discovered that a vessel, bound for Elsinore, was about to leave Kirkcaldy. She was called the *Ayngell*, and the safety of the royal personages was entrusted to her experienced crew. These precautions notwithstanding, this spring crossing was attended by more alarms and excursions at sea than the outward voyage had been in the later season. James firmly believed that the 'incantations of witches' had been the cause of his rough passage and, although no harm had come to the Royal barque, another vessel bringing gifts to the queen was sent to the bottom between Burntisland and the Port.

Disembarking on The Shore at Leith, James and his bride were welcomed by the firing of cannon and the discharging of an equally sonorous loyal address in Latin, after which they proceeded to the King's Wark where all was in readiness for their reception. When the coronation procession arrived in the ancient capital of his race, James rode on horseback, the queen followed in a regal chariot, and the gutters of the Auld Toun ran red with wine for the rude populace from the Mercat Cross.

Charles II, great-grandson of the Queen of Scots, had less pleasant memories of Scotland than had James VI, his grandfather. Proclaimed king in 1649 at the Mercat Cross of Edinburgh (no flowing fount of Bacchus on this occasion) at the age of eighteen, and a week after the execution of Charles I, he was invested with his right to the Scottish crown but not yet to the crown of England, a country destined to be ruled by the Parliamentarians for the next ten years. The crown of the northern kingdom had been forfeited by his father

The King's Wark, the successor to a much larger waterside building, owned by the Stuart kings of Scotland.

because he had refused to accept the National Covenant, and the younger Charles had to make up his mind about the same burning question. It was soon clear to him that, if he wanted to take the crown, he would have to take the Covenant as well, so he allied himself to a cause which he liked, in fact, no better than Charles I had done. This arrangement was unwelcome news in the South, and Cromwell decided to persuade the Scots by force of arms to give up their king. Yet again a warlike host marched northwards but David Leslie, the commander of the Scottish army, had no intention of allowing the Roundheads to get into Leith as this would have given them control of the harbour in which their ships carrying the ever necessary supplies could have anchored safely. As noted in the previous chapter, the victory in this encounter went to the Scots. In the meantime Charles, after his entertainment at a banquet in the Parliament House in Edinburgh in July 1650, 'thairafter went down to Leith to ane ludging belonging to the Lord Balmerinoch' which was placed at his disposal 'during his abyding in Leith'.

Charles was crowned by the Marquis of Argyle at Scone in January 1651, but Leslie's army, after several reverses, was finally defeated at the Battle of Worcester in the following autumn and Leslie himself was taken prisoner. Leaving his crown behind in Scotland, Charles fled abroad, and nine years were to pass before the Restoration of the Monarchy in England made it possible for him to return. With the crown he most coveted now firmly on his head, he instructed Sir William Bruce, his Architect in Scotland, to enlarge and embellish his Palace of Holyroodhouse in Edinburgh, but, scunnered at Scotland by conventicles and covenants, he did not come back to see or live in it. Nor did any of his successors for over one hundred and fifty years, and the crown itself, after the Union of the Parliaments in 1707, lay hidden in a chest in Edinburgh Castle.

If Mary Queen of Scots could dimly have foreseen the future, as perhaps she tried to do from time to time within the confining walls that closed around her so early in her stressful life, it is not impossible that she presaged a prolongation of the Stuart line, and the crown, even the longed-for crown of a united kingdom, being inherited by her heirs, but it is hardly probable that she could have conjured up the scene at Leith when an alien German prince (who was nevertheless a direct descendant of the Queen of Scots) stood upon The Shore to receive a rapturous reception from the descendants of her subjects. Scotland had to await the advent of Sir Walter Scott to bring the king to its capital and rescue the crown from its concealment.

On 15th August 1822 King George IV, on board the *Royal*

George, arrived with escorting frigates in the roads of Leith 'and a salute from the battery announced that all had come to anchor'. Sir Walter was among the first on board to welcome him and was not above putting a souvenir of the occasion in his pocket, a glass from which the former Prince Regent had drunk being conveniently to hand. In his absorption in the proceedings, however, he absent-mindedly sat down, and the glass was crushed to fragments!

A barge brought the king ashore, watched admiringly by probably the largest crowd the port had ever witnessed whose acclamations, being 'all unused to royalty, seemed to rend heaven'. To this tumult of sound was added the firing of ships' cannon and the skirling of pipers on the pier, while 'the combined cheers of the mighty multitude filled up the pauses'. As well he might be, George IV was 'visibly affected' by this display of loyalty, and the success of his one and only state visit to Scotland turned out to be a salutary influence on the manner in which he addressed himself to the art of kingship on his return to London. Hardly a very memorable monarch, he was a slightly more significant one after experiencing such an unearned and unexpected reception in Leith and Edinburgh. But the Scottish crown was never placed upon his head.

George IV's disembarkation at The Shore was depicted on the one-guinea note issued by the Leith Banking Company, with the Custom House in the background. The Bank was founded in 1793 and lasted until 1842. Each note recorded the Banking Company's promise 'to pay the bearer one pound one shilling [£1.05p] on demand at their office in Leith'.

From the ramparts of Edinburgh Castle the king looked out over the new-built houses of the partially completed New Town, the waters of the Firth of Forth and the distant hills, and confessed that he had not known that such a view existed in all his kingdom. It did not fall to Leith, however, to bid him farewell. After a final glittering occasion at Hopetoun House (when he knighted the portrait-painter Henry Raeburn)

The Shore, Leith, from the Victoria Swing Bridge at Leith Docks.
It was here that George IV landed on his famous visit to Scotland
in 1822. The Signal Tower is on the left.

he rejoined the *Royal George* at Port Edgar and sailed south.

These had been very different scenes from sad Mary's homecoming to the pier at Leith, when Knox had never seen so dolorous a face of heaven, but it is the enigma that was Mary that has exercised the minds and the imaginations of every succeeding generation, for the crown never rested on a more tragic or a more romantic head.

CHAPTER ELEVEN

The Port and The Town

The troubles of Leith, frequently lamented by its historians, are of ancient origin, and the blame has been laid squarely at the door of the sister city where, unfortunately, it largely, if not wholly, belongs. They began, presumably unintentionally, in the early years of the 14th century when King Robert the Bruce forged the first link in its chain of servitude by renewing an old grant of the Harbour to the burgesses of Edinburgh. The Bruce charter did not include any right to the banks of the Water of Leith, then, as already mentioned, a larger and deeper waterway than it has since become, and disputes with Sir Robert Logan, to whom the river banks belonged, were not infrequent. The superiority of Leith was in the hereditary possession of the ruthless Logans of Restalrig, a family which played an intermittent and, particularly in the case of the last baron in the long line of Robert Logans at the end of the 16th century, a plotting, scheming role behind the scenes in Scottish history, and whose race stretched back to very early times. Towards the end of the 14th century the Robert Logan of that time married into the family of de Lestalric, thus acquiring Leith as well as the barony later known as Restalrig, and their son married a daughter of Robert II.

As early as 1398 Robert Logan sold to Edinburgh his feudal rights to a piece of land in Leith which gave the city authorities the free access they so much wanted to the river banks. Under this bond, described as 'exclusive, ruinous and enslaving', wharfs and quays were to be built along the banks, granaries and shops erected and roads constructed to meet the growing need for better transport. Taken as its face value, this might have been considered an enlightened civic policy of investment in the future prosperity of Leith, but such a desirable result was far from being the outcome or, for that matter, the intention. Trade was unquestionably to be increased and business to flourish, but, owing to punitive preconditions dictated by the Town, the profits went not to the port which was earning them but to the capital. For the diversion of revenues from Leith there was one principal explanation. The magistrates and town council of Edinburgh gradually obtained the superiority of the whole of Leith, the only exception being Yardheads, which takes its name from the walls bounding the orchards belonging to the canons of St. Anthony's, and the lands of St. Anthony's themselves for both of which the dues were paid to the Kirk Session of South Leith Church: all the rest went to Edinburgh.

The old Preceptory of the canons had been founded about 1430, approximately fifty years earlier than the church originally dedicated to St. Mary. The Preceptory, quite close to which St. Mary's had been built, owed its existence to the Logans and there, in accordance with custom and their own instructions, they were to be 'prayit for ilk Sunday till the day of doom'. About thirty years after the Reformation, by which time the last of the remaining monks had probably died, the monastic funds were made over to St. Mary's which by that time had become South Leith Parish Church. It had been the only foundation of the Order of St. Anthony in Scotland.

The church of St. Mary stood in the Kirkgate opposite Trinity House, the latter built, as already mentioned, in 1555 by the Masters and Mariners of Leith and rebuilt, at a cost of £2,500, in 1816 in a classical style with central pediment and groups of twin columns by the architect Thomas Brown. Trinity House continued to function in its original charitable capacity but in 1797 'it was erected by charter into a corporate body, vested with powers to examine and, under its common seal, to license persons to be pilots, and to exact admission fees from licentiates.' (*Leith and its Antiquities* by J.

Campbell Irons.) Today Trinity House still continues its charitable role but no longer has any involvement in the licensing of pilots.

St. Mary's was not the earliest place of worship for the people of South Leith as Restalrig had been the predominant town with its own church serving the whole area, and it was for the purpose of providing a church in the immediate locality that the Kirkgate site was chosen for the new foundation in the late 15th century. Restalrig Church was desecrated during the Reformation and was only rebuilt in 1838, by William Burn, with a few fragments of the original choir still surviving. The adjoining St. Triduana's Well, also now restored, was a place of pilgrimage for sufferers from diseases of the eyes, the spring of remedial water being enclosed by a vaulted chapel with a central supporting column which has the appearance of a medieval chapter-house.

The trade incorporations had their chapels, which they maintained at their own expense, in St. Mary's and a lamp hung over the statue of Our Lady above the high altar, while the Madona and Child within a canopied galley became incorporated in the arms of the Port of Leith.

The old church in South Leith, its fabric having suffered badly during the turbulent events of earlier years, was rebuilt in 1848 by Thomas Hamilton. It and its burial ground and Trinity House survive beside the Newkirkgate Shopping Centre which dates from 1965. The suburban-style housing, in stark contrast to what it has replaced (which, it must be admitted, was far gone in advanced decrepitude), was completed by 1975.

A prominent but now vanished Kirkgate building was the tavern known as Cant's Ordinary, mine host being Mr Cant, a member of a family then well known in Leith. In explanation of the name of this quaint, archaic edifice with its arcaded frontage, a few lines may be quoted from James Boswell's *Life of Johnson* where the word 'Ordinary' is used in a similar sense: '. . . happening to dine at Clifton's eating house, in

Butcher-row, I was surprised to perceive Johnson come in and take his seat at another table. The mode of dining, or rather being fed, at such houses in London is well known to many to be particularly unsocial, as there is no Ordinary or united company, but each person has his own mess and is under no obligation to hold any intercourse with any one.'

The economic factors were also strongly slanted in Edinburgh's favour, Royal Burghs possessing a monopoly of trading rights over a much wider area than their own boundaries. As a result, no buying and selling could take place in Leith itself but only in the recognised Edinburgh markets and at prices laid down by the City. Marketable commodities could only be assessed and weighed within the Royal Burgh and stent, or tax, was payable on all such goods before they could be offered for sale. Infringement of such laws was not, of course, uncommon, with business being conducted outside the prescribed demarcations and merchandise being 'passed over garden walls' to avoid the dues.

No Leith trader could become a burgess, nor could he enter into partnership with an Edinburgh merchant, and no burgess was permitted to reside in Leith. Those who, by so doing, attempted to evade their responsibilities as 'freemen' while retaining and enjoying their privileges, went in danger of being removed from office. In the year 1580 a 'candil maker' called Thomas Lamb was 'callit and accuset for meltein of tallow in the unfrie toun of Leyth', and anyone discovered buying imported goods directly from the seller was fined for his audacity and had his ill-gotten purchases impounded, as they should first, according to the rules, have been bought by the magistrates and sent to the marketplace in Edinburgh.

The narrow thoroughfare known as Burgess Close was, as its name implied, out of bounds to the unfree men of Leith, and it was here that the counting-houses of the Edinburgh burgesses were located. Leith traders who wished to ship their wares to a foreign port had to pay the appropriate tariff and obtain a licence.

In early times the working life of Leithers was carried out under the aegis of four incorporations, the mariners, the brewers and maltmen, traders (such as coopers, cordiners, bakers and others), and the merchants and shopkeepers, their original charter having been granted by the Logans of Restalrig in the sixteenth century. The members of these incorporations, who could not of course be burgesses, could only protect their interests by erecting monopolies that were as jealously guarded as those of the craft guilds of Edinburgh. This state of affairs was not remedied until 1734 when, by a declaration of their independence from the Town, the Leith traders were no longer referred to as unfree. Each incorporation had originally established an altar to its patron saint in the parish church, and contributions were made by the members towards defraying the costs involved as well as to a much-needed fund for relieving the poor and the infirm.

The Incorporation of Coopers of Leith made common cause with the Fleshers and Masons in upholding the altar of St. John in the New Kirk of St. Mary's. The Sederunt Books of the Coopers, as of other incorporations, are still extant. Their funds were built up by the ingathering of weekly dues from their craftsmen, and strangers taking up booths in the town for the exercise of the craft had to obtain permission to do so and to make payment of the dues and taxes exigible. Those who failed to provide meal for the chaplain were 'poinded' (i.e. had their property confiscated), and fines were imposed on any craftsmen who spoiled their work, which they had to 'mend' at their own expense. In the nineteenth century the Coopers' minute books recorded case after case of hardship and deprivation among their members, and the corporation's carefully considered and frequently reviewed attempts to mitigate them. When an application was received from a member, he was called before their elected representatives and examined as to whether he derived any pecuniary aid from other sources. If his need was deemed genuine, he might be granted such meagre assistance as '3/- [15p] per week but only until next quarter day', or if he were already in receipt of benefit to the extent of 6/- [30p] weekly, he ran the risk of having it reduced to five after a twelvemonth.

The Burlaw Court dealt with matters agricultural which were also of considerable importance to the life of Leith. Corn grew in the fields to landward of the Port, and rules were drawn up by the court to prevent abuses. A proclamation of 1710 prohibited the bringing in of corn after 7 o'clock in the evening after the discovery that it was being 'stollan and embezeled from the fields and brought into this toun under cloud of night'. The ground was sown to a large extent with pease, and pigs, sheep and geese were kept by the farming community. The Burlaw Court was empowered to fine anyone found 'lying doun amongst corn' or 'treading doun and pulling ye complainers pease or turkie beans'. The Court continued its functions until the middle of the eighteenth century and met on the south side of the Links at Duncat, or Dovecot, Yard, weather permitting. On inclement days it was held in Clephane's Tavern.

During the troubled period when Mary of Guise ruled as Queen Regent, she gave an undertaking to erect Leith into a Burgh of Barony as a preliminary to its being raised to the status of a Royal Burgh, and with this end in view she purchased the superiority from Sir Robert Logan for the benefit of the citizenry. This superiority included the Links and placed a still larger area of the Port under the authority of the Town when, to the continuing detriment of Leith, she died a few years after this enlightened step. Her daughter, Mary Queen of Scots, having less reason to show gratitude to the people of the Port, granted the superiority to the City albeit with reluctance. One advantage alone remained from these aborted plans. Leith was now reckoned as a town, having till then counted only as a village.

The few featureless back streets between Bernard Street and Tower Street and still known as Timber Bush are all that remain of the little mercantile enclave in Leith where, and where alone, the Town of Edinburgh countenanced the storing of goods unloaded at the quays. It has a colourful history that is as interestingly instructive about the bygone life of Leith as it is unexpected in so unpromising a place. The unusual name is a corruption of Timber Bourse which at once explains the nature of its use, for it was here that the timber merchants carried on their business which was probably considerable, bearing in mind the large amount of wood required by the wrights and builders. The famous Memel pine, imported from the Baltic, was much in demand. This was no ordinary, run-of-the-mill set of commercial bargaining booths, however. Taking its inspiration, as usual, from the auld ally across the North Sea and, indeed, its name as well, it was a Merchants' Exchange quite in the continental manner. A paved piazza with seats and benches was enclosed by stone arches supported on columns, and it is to be regretted that no trace of this remarkable early 17th-century edifice has survived. It was the brainchild of Bernard Lindsay, Gentleman of the Bedchamber to James VI, whose name is commemorated in Bernard Street. From James he received that other notable pile, the King's Wark (or Work), within a dale's length of the Timber Bush, a much smaller, newer version of which still stands, restored and functioning, at the waterside in spite of a proposal to have its demolished in 1971. The generosity of the Wisest Fool in Christendom would not be over-estimated by those who knew that the favoured recipient had himself had to meet the cost of making good the old structure which was then in need of repair. While he was at it, the King's 'chalmer chiel', who had married Barbara, a daughter of the notorious Logans, decided to make this the 'chief ornament' of Leith, and to enhance its environs he built the piazza and a tennis court on which the king was pleased to demonstrate his skill during his visit to Edinburgh in 1617.

As it stood at the entrance to the Harbour the King's Wark, which had been built for James I, was part of the port's defences and also served the combined purposes of royal arsenal, general warehouse and dwelling apartments for various officials. In 1575 it had been taken over as a hospital for victims of the plague. Although James VI gave Bernard Lindsay permission to keep four taverns in the Wark as well as the tennis court for the now popular game of 'catchpel', he reserved one cellar for himself. This was to be kept in repair for the storage of the king's wines and other provisions. The whole property was conveyed to the Edinburgh magistrates, and in 1649 the tennis court was reconstructed as a weigh-house. In the 1970s the interior of the King's Wark was completely renewed to provide eight flats and a shop. The public house which occupied the ground floor still remains but has been totally reconstructed behind the facade. The most recent alteration was the redevelopment of the Timber Bush area in 1991 by Waverley Properties who discovered, after research into the history of the site, that they had created a modern piazza, consisting of offices and luxury apartments, on the same ground as the old piazza had been built by the stone-masons employed by Bernard Lindsay!

An Admiralty Court was held in the Tolbooth but, losing its maritime functions by degrees, it became eventually a purely civic institution, although the titles of Admiral and Admirals Depute (in the 17th century the duties of the Admiral were carried out by the less pretentiously styled Water Bailie) were used by the Provost and Bailies after 1833 when, as a result of the Reform Act, Leith was granted the status of a Parliamentary Burgh. It had its own Town Council and, by the passing of the Leith Act in 1827, magistrates had been given permission to live in Leith. In 1826 the Town's five hundred-year-old administration of the Harbour came to an end when it was handed over to the Dock Commissioners after another skirmish with the Edinburgh Town Council. The Docks having become bankrupt, a proposal to sell them together with the Harbour to a joint stock company, the profits of which would be used to repay the dockland debts, seemed to offer a convenient solution. This was, however, one instance when the Town failed in its exploitation of the Port and, in Lord Cockburn's words, 'fell into a pit dug by itself'. Some members of the council were discovered to have bought shares for their own personal gain and, the trustees having therefore sold their own entrusted property to themselves, the whole scheme was summarily abandoned.

The Port had got its freedom from the Town at last. Its consequent prosperity was such that from 1871 to 1881 the population increased by more than 13,000. But its freedom was to be short-lived. With the extension of the Edinburgh boundaries in 1920 Leith was brought, having fought hard to

Above the waters of Lochend Loch stands a fragment of the old stronghold of the Logans of Restalrig, Lochend House.

retain its independence, within the confines of the city, when its long-awaited and much-prized Town Council ceased to exist.

The decisive part played by the Logans of Restalrig in the history of Leith came to an abrupt end during the reign of James VI. The last Sir Robert Logan became a participant in that strange enigma in Scotland's annals, the Gowrie Conspiracy. His part, as much surrounded by mystery as the other aspects of that extraordinary drama, was discovered after his death, and it was in macabre keeping with this curious

John's Place, a delightful example of the short-lived Georgian development in Leith and for many years a favourite choice for foreign consulates in the Port.

episode that his bones were exhumed and put on trial in 1609. A sentence of forfeiture was passed on Logan's skeleton, but it is on record that this was reversed a few years later. On the clifftop above Lochend Loch a fragment of his old fortified house overhangs the water. Seen from the other side, it is less impressive as a large extension was built on to it during the early 19th century, but a massive chimney dominates the rubble-built fragment, the earliest part of which dates from the 16th century. It was here, in the old house, that the ultimate baron of the Logan line is said to have clung, as far as his diminished resources would allow, to the last vestiges of feudal pomp, while plotting secretly to out-plot the king who was secretly plotting to obtain the throne of England!

Cockburn's comments on the old and bitter feud between the Port and the Town were blunt and to the point. They had both been intemperate and unreasonable, he said, and 'if Leith had the advantage in coarse violence, Edinburgh was compensated by its superiority in disdainful insolence . . . . The true value of the affair lay in its aiding the growth of independence in Leith'.

CHAPTER TWELVE

An Edinburgh
Transport Museum

The former Edinburgh Transport Museum at Shrubhill on
Leith Walk was well worth a visit, particularly as its subsequent closure was heralded during its last year or two by a general air of neglect within the four walls of the comparatively
small area in which a few fascinating examples of the city's
former public transport conveyances were displayed, and the
time in which they could be seen together as a collection was
therefore running out.

On entering, the first vehicles to meet the eye were likely to
be a few parked cars, but these unexpected intruders were
soon forgotten in the absorbing interest of the exhibits themselves. The earliest and most visually pleasing was a horse-
drawn car, painted black and yellow, which had plied, as its
route-board still announced, from Albert Street, via Elm Row
and Easter Road, to London Road. Tracks had been laid in
Edinburgh and Leith, then a separate burgh, after the passing
of the Tramways Act in 1870, and the first horse cars, replac-
ing the older horse buses which had in their turn replaced the
earlier stage coaches, were in operation by the end of the following year. The system, when fully developed, was to service
eighteen miles of route with ninety trams and one hundred
and ten horses, the drivers working sixty-nine hours each
week for which they were paid exactly twenty shillings (£1). A
minimum of two horses was required for these cars, but four
or five were needed for some routes, and a trace horse was
necessary on the city's many steep hills. There was competi-

tion for the job of 'trace boy'. The enviable task of these small boys was to ride the extra horse downhill again when the long upward climb had been successfully negotiated.

In the horse tram preserved in the museum the passengers sat on long bench-like seats, facing each other, inside, or on the six double ones on the open top, and the driver mounted to his 'box' by means of two well spaced out steps; even the whip was still to be seen placed conveniently to his hand. 'Edinburgh and District Tramways Company Ltd.' is attractively lettered along both sides of the car, together with the name 'John E. Pitcairn, General Manager'. Mr Pitcairn's term of office coincided with the changeover from horse-drawn to cable tramcars, and he superintended the forging of that particular link in the chain of successive vehicles and methods which tell the story of the transport history of Edinburgh. When examples were being sought for restoration and exhibition in the museum, this splendid old horse tram was discovered, and rescued from a perilous plight of deterioration, in Tranent where it was in use as a chicken run!

Among several small-scale reproductions in the building were models of the cable haulage system, of a Shrubhill-built tramcar which was the forerunner of the standard Edinburgh Corporation Transport cars operating through the streets from 1934 to the 1950s, and of a cable car, on loan from the Royal Scottish Museum, indicating the ownership of the original to have been the 'Patent Cable Tramway Corporation Limd.' Many of these cable cars were later converted for use with the subsequent electric system. The museum's own representative of the cable-car era was almost as attractive as the old horse tram and, indeed, the later history of transport illustrates the parallel aesthetic decline which tends to accompany technological advance in this and most other fields. Still with an open top, the platform at each end is closed at the side opposite the entrance by a wrought-iron scrollwork panel, and this is complemented by a similar painted design in black on the narrow, rounded sides of the window frames. These ornamental features symbolise a vanished craftsmanship and personal pride in a well-finished product not likely soon, if ever, to be revived.

Cable trams were running in the city from 1888 onwards, but by the early years of the 20th century the underground mechanism, driven by power stations at four different locations, was becoming worn, delays and breakdowns were increasingly frequent and frustrating, and there was growing public dissatisfaction. This was not, however, the case in Leith, which had wisely exchanged its horse trams for an overhead electric traction system, with the result that passengers from Edinburgh had to 're-embark' at Pilrig Street, where the cables terminated, for the rest of their journey. As a consequence this route was the first to be converted when Edinburgh itself 'went electric', and it was opened on 20th June 1922 for passengers travelling between Pilrig and Liberton. A contemporary photograph shows a huge crowd worthy of a Lord Mayor's Show assembled at the time-honoured Leith and Edinburgh boundary at Pilrig to witness the historic event, a number of students having scrambled onto the roof of the (now enclosed) upper portion of the tram for a free ride. The power station for cable cars on the North Side was in Henderson Row.

Like Lothian Road, said to have been constructed in a single day over a hundred years earlier, Princes Street was relaid with, albeit temporary, tracks for electric tramcars in a single night, the work also including the setting up of central poles and overhead wiring. By 1927 345 electric cars were running in Edinburgh, which had of course included Leith since the boundary extension of 1920.

For tarring the road surfaces the Corporation had its own steam rollers, and the museum was fortunate in having, and displaying, a splendidly conserved example repainted in its original colours of red and black. Massive, heavy and of iron construction, these service vehicles lumbered slowly and noisily along the streets on their enormous wheels, smoke issuing from their tall, black frontal chimneys, like mobile furnaces, which is what in essence they were. To be seen at their best, they had to be seen in action, but the retired veteran in the transport collection was impressive enough with its iron rake and shovel hanging in readiness towards the rear and a cast brass figure of Britannia clutching her trident above a crouching lion providing the only, and wholly appropriate, decoration at the front. The one thing missing was the pungent smell of tar!

The interior, however, was not so easily examined, although the levers and handles on the firebox, dated 1910, were reasonably visible. The boiler was another matter, however, and the metal notice which it carried to the effect that it must be cleaned thoroughly after every hundred hours of working and that oil and grease must on no account be allowed to get inside, could only be read by the exercise of some physical dexterity, a problem explained by the necessity of preventing visitors from entering the vehicles as they had not always been treated in the past with due respect!

Round the museum's walls hung a series of photographs depicting transport evolution in the city, one showing a First World War conductress standing on her platform beneath a huge advertisement for H. P. Sauce. The advertisements in these old photographs ranged from the familiar Bovril and Colman's Mustard to such outdated products as black lead and Rising Sun Stove Polish. 'Graveyard of the Electric Tramway System' was the caption under one which portrayed cars being scrapped by a contractor, and another showed the gaily decorated tram which was the last one to be seen in Edinburgh bearing the legend 'The Last Tram Week' and the relevant dates of 1871 and 1956. Tram drivers' wages at various periods were given among the printed information. In 1950 they earned 2/7½d (about 13p) an hour for a forty-hour week! As they ran on electricity the trams did not pollute the environment and their abandonment was probably a major error on the part of the authorities.

While engrossed in the interest generated by the museum collection the telltale signs of dereliction could easily be ignored, but when coming suddenly on a shelf, badly in need of repainting, labelled 'Visitors Book' from which that item was conspicuously missing, it was impossible not to wonder how long ago it had disappeared and what the date of the last entry might have been.

But this was not an old and wornout building and had in fact been purpose-built as a transport museum. Its problems, caused largely by a roof that had been badly designed, had developed fairly quickly and by 1982 its demolition had become an urgent necessity. Of primary concern was the safe removal of the vehicles, but no alternative could be found to their dispersal. The electric tram No. 35 was sent to Blackpool and from there to Glasgow where it provided visitor-conveyance at the Garden Festival in 1988, its final 'terminus' being the National Tramway Museum in Derbyshire. The destination of the venerable old horse-drawn bus was the Commercial Transport Museum in Lancashire, while the setting up of the Scottish Vintage Bus Museum at Lathalmond, in Fife, guaranteed a suitable sanctuary for buses which had been running in Edinburgh between 1948 and 1977. The small exhibits have been stored in the hope that it may be possible for another museum of transport to be opened. Like the re-establishment of a Leith Museum, however, this would not appear to be likely in the foreseeable future.

CHAPTER THIRTEEN

Landward Leith

Before the North Bridge was built in the second half of the eighteenth century, the journey to Leith from Old Edinburgh on its ridge of rock was a daunting and hazardous undertaking. The precipitous northern slope of the ridge, at the foot of which lay the valley between it and the Calton Hill which corresponded with the Cowgate valley on the other or southern side, had first to be negotiated and, to facilitate an easier access to the Port, the steep, descending street known as Leith Wynd was consequently constructed. It was in fact a continuation, across the High Street, of St. Mary's Wynd which climbed the hill from the south, the Netherbow Port, which marked the boundary between the city and the separate burgh of Canongate, standing at the junction of the two thoroughfares. The cross streets followed the line of an ancient Roman road.

At the bottom of Leith Wynd, on opposite sides of the street, stood the Trinity College Church and Hospital founded in 1462 by Mary of Gueldres, Queen of James II, and the old charitable workhouse known as Paul's Work erected by the city magistrates in 1479 when, according to contemporary records, sterner methods were used to persuade 'ydill people to betake themselves to sum Vertew and Industrie' than are deemed appropriate now. Paul's Work, founded by Bishop Spence of Aberdeen and dedicated to the Virgin, was afterwards used for the unlikely twin purposes of a woollen manufactory and a house of correction. This old and picturesque group of buildings was sacrificed to the North British Railway in the nineteenth century, although part of the Trinity

Church was re-erected near the Old Town on higher and safer ground below the ridge. Through the gate, or port, which closed the Wynd at this point, the burgh of Calton was entered at its principal street, St. Ninian's or, significantly, Beggars' Row, where for long had stood beside the way the chapel dedicated to St. Ninian. A narrow lane or close known as the Salt Backet ran off St. Ninian's Row and in it another chapel, a small Methodist meeting-house standing, says Grant, 'almost in the direct line of the Regent Arch' in Waterloo Place on the hillside above, was built by the Wesleyans. The Row skirted the Hill and its outcrops which were then devoid of monuments.

The Barony of Calton or Caldtoun was owned in the seventeenth century by Lord Balmerino, of the Elphinstone family, who in the same century purchased the building, afterwards known as Balmerino House, in which Charles II had found lodging in the Kirkgate of Leith during his 'Scottish adventure' of 1650 when he had little choice but to support the Presbyterian cause in order to restore the monarchy in Scotland. The Church of Our Lady Star of the Sea was built in the grounds of Balmerino House in 1853. As time has told, it was with Leith that the history of the Burgh of Calton – a name which had many variants including Craigend, Craigingalt and Galttoun – was to be most closely linked. A charter of 1725 reveals that the lands of Calton, Back of Canongate and Yardheads of Leith, having been part of the Barony of Restalrig, were at that date made over to the Burgh of Edinburgh. The origin of the name Craigend is of some interest. In the Middle Ages the parish of South Leith encompassed a loch, the water of which was later used to provide the houses of Leith with their first supply of piped water, and a craig or hill. The loch end of the parish became known as Lochend, and Craigend was the name given to the other end of the parish at the Calton Hill.

About 1945 a short history of 'the Calton' was written by a well-known 'indweller', as he called himself, Mr Francis Caird

Inglis, who succeeded his father in the long line of pioneer photographers at Rock House on the Calton Hill which had started in the 1840s with David Octavius Hill, whose early calotypes are so much prized today. Quoting from the Parish Registers of South Leith, he tells how, in 1643, a bailie and elders from 'Lastelrig [Restalrig] and Caldtoune' were ordained to 'take up a list of ye fencible persones' in both localities, a reference to the efforts then being made by the Scottish Church to enlist in the Covenanting Army all those who were capable of bearing firearms. The Covenant was sworn 'by both man and woman' as a congregation in December 1648, and on Christmas Eve intimation was made that they should come to 'subscrive ye same' the following Tuesday 'after sermon'. Before the advent of newspapers it was common practice for items of local and national interest to be intimated from parish pulpits, the latter often to inform the people of Acts which had been passed by Parliament.

Almost twenty years later the members of South Leith Church were reminded of their 'Saboth day' instructions in a report from the Presbytery read out by the minister. 'No boats barks or any uyr vessells' should 'sail out the harbour upon the Lord's day under paine of censur both civil and ecclesiastick', no persons should be found drawing water from the wells and carrying it to their houses, and no-one must 'vaige' upon the shore 'efter ye afternoon's sermon' or in any street in Restalrig or Craigend 'under paine of lyk censur'.

By 1674 the steeple was in need of 're-edifying', and the concurrence in an appeal for contributions towards its repair was sought from the Session and the Laird of Craigentinnie, who at that time was either Sir Patrick Nisbet, who had been created a baronet of Nova Scotia in 1669 (the ground now covered by the Castle Esplanade having been 'converted' into the soil of that country for the purpose of selling baronetcies), or his second cousin, Alexander, with whom he exchanged the estate of Craigentinnie for that of Dean. In 1682, to settle a quarrel, Alexander Nisbet left the country, and on his return was promptly imprisoned in the Tolbooth, together with his opponent, for taking part in a duel.

In 1695 permission was given, surprisingly, for the inhabitants of Calton to 'bury ye dead' upon 'ye Sabath'. They might do so, 'if they please', between sermons, provided that in winter they were at the churchyard 'before two hours chap in ye clock of South Leith'.

There is an amusing entry in the records of July 1696. It had become a practice in the reformed church in Scotland, when they were not in use, to lock the box-seats of those members who were of substance in the community, and an official pew-opener with sets of keys was always in attendance before services. The key-keeper 'of ye Caltoun seats' appears to have abused his office by refusing to open the pews of certain gentlemen until after 'Sermon was begun' because they 'would not give him money'. For this offence he was appointed 'to be summoned to ye Session'.

The Barony of Calton had its own Baron Bailie and its honorary constables from whom subsequently developed the Society of High Constables of Calton in the early nineteenth century. It had also the right to hold its own Beltane Day celebrations which took place each year in early May and over which the Baron Bailie presided attired in his robes and badge of office. For the enforcement of law and order in the district the Calton drummer, when occasion demanded it, went sounding through the streets with civic proclamations, one such occasion in 1772 being for the purpose of dissuading the local apprentices from throwing stones and mobbing, and another four years later being in order 'to prevent persons from bickering on the Calton hill'. His remuneration for carrying out this duty was two shillings (10p). Public services of this nature were probably in frequent demand, as repairs to 'the Calton drum' became necessary around this time. In 1816 the burgh acquired an association with the 'immortal memory' when Burns' Clarinda, Mrs Maclehose, went to live on the upper floor of a tenement house, now demolished, in the little street called Calton Hill.

This was an area rich in natural springs, and its indwellers were consequently much more easily supplied with water than the inhabitants of the Old Town itself, who were hard put to it to keep the dirty closes and the high, over-populated 'lands' in any state approaching cleanliness.

'Until Waterloo Place and Regent's Bridge' – the former to commemorate the victorious battle of 1815 and the latter to compliment the Prince Regent who later entered Edinburgh by this route as George IV – 'were opened', wrote John Geddie, 'the Calton Hill was reached by descending into the depths of Low Calton and climbing up the steep and narrow path of Craigend.' The new roadway to the east was driven through the Calton burial ground as relentlessly as a few years later the railway ironware of the Age of Steam was to be thrust through the quiet hollow in which were situated Paul's Work and the Trinity College Church, the remnants of St. Ninian's Chapel being destroyed when the ground was cleared for the building of the Regent's Arch. Leith Wynd itself, overtaken by the tide of nineteenth-century redevelopment and 'improvement', became the site, to quote the same historian of Edinburgh, of 'railway platforms, sidings and signal boxes'. Geology being more impervious to change than the works of man, only the rocks and the everlasting hills remain.

CHAPTER FOURTEEN

Perils of the Port

In the year 1622, in the first week of June, there were alarms and excursions in the port of Leith. Three foreign ships 'in the heart of Leith harbour', as James Grant describes the incident, were varying by a sea-fight the usual 'excitements of the times'. At this period the mutual enmity between Spain and Holland was so strong that the presence together in a neutral port of Dutch and Spanish ships could lead to a dangerous confrontation which the port authorities were hard put to it to control.

The Spanish frigate was about peaceful purposes enough. Being in no hurry to take on board their required provisions, the crew went ashore as they felt inclined. But when two 'vessels of War', commanded by the Admiral of Zealand, anchored alongside them, the situation changed quickly and dramatically for the worse during a night which would not soon be forgotten in the Port. At dawn the battle of the boats was causing such 'terror and confusion' among the inhabitants that the burgesses 'rushed to arms and armour' and, although the Water Bailie accompanied by a herald commanded 'both parties to forbear hostilities in Scottish waters', attack and counter-attack 'continued with unabated fury until midnight'.

The Spanish captain, having at his disposal the artillery of one ship only, got the worst of it as the 'Dutchmen poured their broadsides upon his shattered hull', and even that tough old race of seadogs the mariners of Leith were, as one authority reported, 'altogether unable . . . to enforce obedience'. The burgesses were now obliged to bring 'ordonance from the

Castell to the shoare to ding at them'. Cannoniers with a battery of guns came down with all speed 'by the Bonnington Road most probably' but arrived too late to save the Spaniards who had been bombarded out of the harbour where their vessel ran aground 'after great slaughter' on the Black Rocks, 'then known as the Mussel Cape'. A party of Leith seamen went on board and raised the Scottish flag, hoping that the Dutch would at least have some respect for the emblem of sovereign authority, but it had no effect: the truculent Dutchmen 'boarded her in the night, burned her to the water's edge, and sailed away before dawn'. (Other accounts place this sea-battle within a longer time-scale than Grant's version allows for.)

Fortunately incidents of such immediate danger were the exception rather than the rule, but Leith has experienced her full share of storm and skaith throughout the stirring years of history.

The Siege of Leith during the Wars of the Reformation, when the Lords of the Congregation, assisted by the Protestant English, turned their force of arms against the Catholic Queen Regent, supported by the French, in the beleaguered Port, threw up perils in plenty for the luckless population. A hundred years later, in the mid-17th century, when Cromwell, after the Battle of Dunbar, succeeded in taking control of Edinburgh and Leith, he delegated to General Monk the task of strengthening the port's defences. So Monk built the Citadel 'benorth the brig' from the bastions of which, however, few guns were ever fired in anger. The later Napoleonic Wars at the end of the 18th century threatened much greater havoc with the prospect of a French invasion. To defend the Harbour entrance a stone Martello tower (now on reclaimed land in the Docks area) was constructed at a cost of £17,000 on the same Mussel Cape rocks that had seen the final undoing of the Old Spanish frigate. The name of these towers, erected along the east coast at this period, was a corruption of Mortella Point in Corsica where a similar

The Martello Tower at Leith, built at sea and now on reclaimed land at the Docks.

defensive structure had withstood a British cannonade in 1794.

The sea itself was a continuing hazard, especially in fogs and storms, and it was not until well into the 19th century that efficient and reliable lights were placed in the Forth for the guidance of shipping which was obliged to pay a levy known as 'light money' to defray their cost. As early as the first half of the 17th century coal lights burned first on the May and then on other islands (but were often mistaken for fires at limekilns and pits on land) and oil lights with rotating and reflecting glasses were not in use until the first years of the 19th century. The merchants of the port contributed £150 towards the cost of erecting a beacon on the Bell Rock in 1803, but it was swept away by gales in the ensuing winter. Lighthouses were expensive and dangerous to build, and progress was held back by lack of funds.

As in all large ports, there was a constant risk of importing infectious disease from foreign crews and insanitary vessels until late in the 19th century, and Leith was fortunate in escaping lightly from the ever-present danger of epidemic outbreaks. An alarming and unexpected warning of these possibilities occurred as late as 1905 when a labourer employed by the Corporation, his wife and their two children were found to be suffering from plague. The woman worked for a rag dealer in squalid premises but the source of the illness was never definitely traced. Though the rest of his family recovered, and no-one else appears to have been affected, the labourer died in Pilton Isolation Hospital, more familiar today as the Northern General. The last and most virulent visitation of Bubonic plague to Edinburgh and Leith in epidemic proportions was in 1645 when 2736 people died in the Port, more than half the population. John Russell writes of the 'terror and distress in Leith', with 'death and desolation in every street', as the previous harvest had failed, and the dreaded 'pest', as it was called, usually followed famine. An attempt was made to cleanse the filth from the streets. Dead swine and the contents of middens were taken in carts to the sands and placed within reach of the tide. On the Links 'great trenches' were dug to receive mass burials, and the remains of these plague victims have been discovered from time to time ever since when the foundations of new buildings have been laid, especially near Wellington Place where the greatest number were interred. For a whole year the people suffered the ravages of this dire disease which had started in April. It abated somewhat in the cold of the succeeding winter but reappeared spasmodically until, with the coming again of Spring in the following year, it finally died away at the end of the most desperate twelve months in the history of Leith. A pair of inscribed silver cups was presented to South Leith Church by the two bailies 'in tyme of pest', and these thank offerings are still in regular use.

Cholera and typhoid fever were both periodic causes of concern. The ravages of cholera on an epidemic scale in Edinburgh and Leith were last experienced in 1866, and typhoid or enteric fever gradually decreased as science and the twentieth century advanced.

In October 1866 the efforts of authority to contain the menacing cholera outbreak met with an astonishingly fatalistic response from the community. The neighbours of those who had died from the disease would not be deterred from crowding into their houses, presumably to condole with remaining relatives, and when remonstrated with by an official, one of them is said to have replied, 'Do you think you can stop the hands of the Almighty? If our time has come you cannot prevent us from being seized'. The first Medical Officer of Health in Edinburgh, Dr, later Sir, Henry Duncan Littlejohn, had been appointed in 1862, and the *Leith Burghs Pilot*, which responsibly reported the course of the epidemic, noted that, in the doctor's opinion, this attitude showed 'not only an amount of ignorance but a degree of recklessness that all must deplore'. It put on record the new Health official's urgent plea for volunteers to undertake a house-to-house visitation in Leith, one of the areas where the outbreak was most severe, in order to 'lead the people to have better ideas on this subject'.

Contraction of the disease was largely confined to the poorer parts of the city, and as clothing purchased from pawnbrokers was considered particularly liable to spread infection, the 'more respectable' pawnbrokers in the Port were interviewed 'to see what could be done in that respect'. Curiously, another dangerous practice was thought to be 'the use of hard ale', and 'its sale had been given up by every respectable establishment in Leith'. One vendor who had been in the Port for thirteen years told how he 'had seen his customers rapidly dying since cholera came to Leith', all 'apparently strong and healthy men'.

Even the vagrants were a menace to the law-abiding working inhabitants to whom they importunately appealed for charity. In South Leith in early times the genuine beggars were given numbered badges to distinguish them from their fraudulent counterparts and were thus licensed to beg unhindered so long as they did not 'cross the bridge' to the Rude Side, at which point the writ of South Leith Church Kirk Session, who authorised and provided the badges, ceased to run. They also appointed a staffman 'to hold the sturdy beggars out of ye towne' but were never entirely successful in ridding the parish of these idle vagabonds who went about in gangs and knew only too well how to 'exercise the wits of the authorities' while continuing to live satisfactorily on their own.

As late as the opening years of the twentieth century the lot of the poor was still a hard and often a hopeless one. In 1909 the *Leith Observer* announced an enquiry into the system of punishment at the Poorhouse, declaring it to be 'a scandal on the part of any efficient Parish Council to send a man to break stones in a close cell at Seafield'. Such places were now to be properly ventilated following a recent incident in which a cell door had been broken down for air by its incarcerated inmate, for which offence he had humanely been let off. It was apparently considered 'that breaking stones was not a punishment but a recognised system of testing cases', and as the man had had over thirty Police Court convictions, he was therefore a test case. Eight recipients of Poorhouse 'charity' had in one afternoon preferred to leave rather than endure conditions created within the cells by ventilation of the kind provided by a quarter-inch space between the closed door and the ground!

The perils of life in the Port were not all of the dire and solemn variety – though small offences were liable to be countered by swift punishments much too stern to fit the crime or the criminals who were often motivated by deprivation and genuine need. On one occasion, prompted by either need or greed, a thief stole the watch-coat in a watch-house from a sleeping watchman, and those invested with the power to mete out justice left the culprit in no doubt about his fate if he were apprehended. He was to be summarily hanged in the watch-house and consigned to the graveyard at South Leith Church. There is no record of the sentence being carried out, but there is of a watchdog being placed in the watch-house to watch the watchmen and their watch-coats, and of an undertaking to keep a most extraordinary and vigilant watch in future inside the watch-house!

The supernatural was sometimes blamed for nocturnal terrors, even when aided and abetted by the demon drink, and there were those who would rather spend a night in the churchyard than walk down St. Anthony's Lane of a dark winter evening. It was here that Green Jenny used to haunt the passers-by till their blood ran cold, and they could never forget the night when the shoemaker, as he himself had recounted it, had left a tavern in the Kirkgate and come face to face in St. Anthony's Lane with a mortcloth standing on end. This was a singular spectacle no doubt, but he had no intention of being frightened of 'twa-three yairds o' green velvet'. The next moment he was completely enveloped by it and, as it smelled undeniably of the charnel-house, shook it off as best he could with trembling hands. Suddenly, standing in front of him, he found a beautiful angel, but the worthy citizen had had enough and took to his heels, which soon carried him out of St. Anthony's Lane.

But Jenny was flesh and blood no less than the shoemaker. Her husband was a brewer in a small way of business who had had the misfortune to become bankrupt but had also had the blessing of a shrewd and hard-working wife. She laboured early and late at the brewery in St. Anthony's Lane, preserving it, when he was 'roupit', from the creditors who were eventually repaid in full. Dressed in a long, white apron over which she threw a large velvet cloak of many folds, she kept a watchful eye on the business premises at night. After her death there were no more ghosts in the Lane, and the solid denizens of Leith could return unhaunted, if still unsteadily, to their homes.

During the Second World War Leith Docks were singled out as a potential target by the German Air Force. In 1940 and 1941 there were several deaths and injuries in the Port as a result of bombs falling in George Street, Portland Place and a site near Leith Hospital, which was fortunately undamaged, as were the Docks themselves.

The last decade or two have witnessed the appearance of an alarming amount of dereliction in Leith due to the wiping out of buildings, many of them dwellinghouses, on a scale far greater than might have been expected from an air raid. The enemy this time was within, when lack of foresight combined with lack of funds to bring about the planning blight which has so harmfully affected Leith and the South Side of Edinburgh. The rebuilding of the Port is producing if not its perils, at least its pressures and its problems, and it is earnestly to be hoped that Leith does not lose any more of its historic personality in the process.

CHAPTER FIFTEEN

Poets of the Port

Like Oxford with her dreaming spires, Edinburgh City, New and Old, the Modern Athens, the Northern Temple of the Winds, has never suffered the neglect of poets. It was Scott's 'own romantic town', Tennyson's 'grey metropolis of the north' and the 'fair city' of Allan Ramsay. But Leith of the sea and the ships that do business in the great waters, as the ancient carved stone declares from the walls of Trinity House, in the Kirkgate, has not by any means been bypassed by the Muse.

Robert Fergusson, whose genius flowered briefly and ended tragically in the City, is well-known for his poems on the Port. His comic celebration of 'Leith Races', using various local dialects of the old Scots language, vividly describes an obviously familiar and highly relished experience in suitably robust rhyme. The first verses set the scene and then he goes on to capture in a colourful word-picture the public holiday atmosphere among the crowd making its noisy, high-spirited way to Leith:

> Quo' she, I ferly unco sair,
> That ye sud musin gae;
> Ye who hae sung o' Hallow-fair,
> Her Winter's pranks, and play;
> Whan on Leith sands the racers rare
> Wi' Jocky louns are met,
> Their orra pennies there to ware,
> And drown themselves in debt,
> Fu' deep that day.

. . .

> We'll reel and ramble thro' the sands,
> And jeer wi' a' we meet;
> Nor hip the daft and gleesome bands
> That fill Edina's street
>   Sae thrang this day.

. . .

> Ere servant-maids had wont to rise
> To seethe the breakfast kettle,
> Ilk dame her brawest ribbons tries,
> To put her on her mettle.

. . .

> Here is the true and faithfu' list
> O' Noblemen and Horses;
> Their eild, their weight, their height, their grist,
> That rin for plates or purses
>   Fu' fleet this day.

The Town Guard, their uniforms and themselves well washed and brushed for the occasion, are much in evidence and proud of their reponsibility for the safe arrival of the purse for which there will later be fierce and exuberant competition:

> To town guard drum of clangour clear,
> Baith men and steeds are raingit;
> Some liveries red or yellow wear,
> And some are tartan spraingit.

The games and excitements, the shrill voices of the ale-wives and the Aberdeen fish sellers and the whole boisterous spectacle are all recorded as if they had taken place the day before, and then, the long-anticipated hours of freedom and amusement over for another year, the homeward exodus from Leith gets under way:

> The races ower, they hale the dools
> Wi' drink o' a kinkind;
> Great feck gae hirplin hame, like fools,
> The cripple lead the blind.

177

The races continued to be held for almost a hundred years after Fergusson's time, but by 1862 they were over for good. The racecourse on the sands then became the site of the Albert Dock, which was opened in 1869, thirteen years after the Victoria Dock, obliterating 84 acres of the sea shore.

Fergusson is best known for his vernacular poetry and his eulogies on ardent spirits, but he wrote in English as well in the approved eighteenth-century style and even devoted an entire poem to the praise of tea. But his lively pen and livelier mind were active for only a few brief years; he died, aged 24, in the miserable and squalid old Bedlam, near the Bristo Port in Edinburgh, and it was reaction to the wretched circumstances of his death that led Professor Andrew Duncan to open a new, humanitarian institution for the mentally ill at Morningside, when the old prison-like, forbidding Bedlam was done away with. Fergusson was buried in the Canongate Churchyard, and it was Robert Burns, in acknowledgement of his debt to the earlier bard, who had a stone placed above the unmarked grave at his own expense.

As a local poet Edinburgh has claimed Fergusson as her own, but it is perhaps not widely remembered now that Leith has her own particular poet as well in the person of Robert Gilfillan, copies of whose work (inferior, it must be said, to that of Fergusson) are rarely come across today. He was not a native of the Port, having been born in 1798 in Dunfermline, but he became resident there later and was appointed Collector of Police Rates in Leith. He died in 1850, and a monumental stone to his memory, says John Russell, was placed in South Leith Churchyard.

In 1831 his *Original Songs*, dedicated to Allan Cunningham – a fellow-poet and the 'honest Allan' of Sir Walter Scott – were published by, among others, James Burnet of Leith. In the introduction to his collected works he claimed to 'enter the lists as no competitor to Burns, Tannahill or MacNeill, but merely as a humble follower – not as a belted earl but as a 'lowly squire'. Had a better education been available to him, he thought, 'the work would probably have presented fewer inelegancies of language'. On the subject of Leith itself, he wrote a parody called 'The Half-Drowned Tar':

> Along by the banks of Leith's ancient harbour
> Jack Oakum reeled drunk from a dive on the shore,
> O' whither, they cried, dost thou steer so to larboard?
> When plump, from the quay-side he quickly fell o'er!

After managing to grab a rope, Jack was pulled from the water. Though his purse was no longer 'with sovereigns full swimming' that he'd 'earned in the war', his rescuers 'hied him away to a tavern' but could not persuade the landlord to draw him rum without payment. Jack had sufficient strength left to floor both them and the landlord, all of whom promptly 'ran like the devil from the half-drowned tar'.

Gilfillan seems to have had a particular bent for writing parody, and the famous 'Blue Bonnets' inspired his verses in praise of Sir Walter Scott:

> Read, read, Woodstock and Waverley,
> Turn every page and read forward in order;
> Read, read, every tale cleverly,
> All the old novels are over the border!

It was the great Battle of 1815, however (at which time he was only 17 years old and may perhaps have written the lines at a later date) that drew from the Poet of Leith, who was favourably mentioned in the renowned *Noctes Ambrosianae* – a fact which must have given him considerable satisfaction – his most stirring verses:

> The trump of war hath ceased to blow,
> And Britain hath no more a foe;
> The sword is sheathed that Scotia drew,
> That gleamed so red on Waterloo.
> That morn, unclouded, rose the sun,
> Our army, too, in brightness shone;

But night displayed another view,
When all was still on Waterloo.

. . .

The trumpet sounds, but ne'er again
Shall Scotia's warriors hear the strain;
They sleep, but not on their mountains blue,
The heroes' bed is Waterloo!
Britannia weeps for many a son,
And a wail is heard in Caledon
For the gallant youths, so brave and true,
Who, fighting, fell on Waterloo!

A less well-known poet was John Logan. Born in 1748 at Soutra where his father was a small farmer, he took orders in the Established Church, was soon a popular preacher and in 1773 was called to South Leith Church. He wrote some of the *Translations and Paraphrases*, which were incorporated in the Hymn Book and called the *Paraphrases*, as part of a plan for the revision of the Psalmody authorised by the General Assembly of the Church of Scotland and published in 1781. 'O God of Bethel' was one of those contributed by Logan, who became one of the minor poets of Scotland with a published collection of poems one of which, *To the Cuckoo*, found its way into a school poetry book in the 1930s in spite of there being some doubt as to its authorship. Of this poem the first and last verses are

Hail, beauteous stranger of the grove!
    Thou messenger of Spring!
Now Heaven repairs thy rural seat,
    And woods thy welcome ring.

O could I fly, I'd fly with thee!
    We'd make, with joyful wing,
Our annual visit o'er the globe,
    Companions of the Spring.

180

Logan also wrote a tragedy and, like John Home the author of *Douglas*, had to resign his charge because of prejudice against theatrical performances. As a consequence he went to London where he contributed to periodical journals. In 1788 he was employed to write a pamphlet entitled A *Review of the Principal Charges against Warren Hastings* (1732–1818–the first Governor-General of India) which resulted in a prosecution of the publisher. The jury, however, found nothing libellous and acquitted the defendant. But John Logan did not live to hear the verdict as he died on 28th December 1788 aged 39.

CHAPTER SIXTEEN

Famous Sons of Leith

An Edinburgh historian whose name is not as well known now as it used to be is Hugo Arnot, a conspicuous eccentric character in the city in the eighteenth century. His father was a shipmaster in Leith called Pollock, and Robert Chambers, in his *Traditions of Edinburgh*, states that he took the name of Arnot from a small inheritance in Fife. His son was acclaimed as a chronicler in 1779 when his *History of Edinburgh* was published, a work which was written when he was under 30 years of age. In 1772 he had entered at the bar and, in the Edinburgh of the 1780s, was the only advocate then residing in the New Town. His house was in Meuse Lane, off St. Andrew Street, where he lived with a manservant during the last few years of his foreshortened life. He was a victim of asthma and a chronic cough which he suspected would one day carry him off like a rocket, which in fact it did, at the age of 37, in 1786.

Poor Hugo's illness was responsible for his having an extremely irritable disposition which tended to exasperate some of his associates, and it was on account of this that he found it necessary to place the prospectuses, or preliminary notices, for another literary work, his *Criminal Trials*, in the coffee houses to bring them to the attention of the public, as the booksellers would have nothing to do with them. His skeletal appearance was the subject of much legal leg-pulling, and John Geddie has preserved one example which was often quoted at the time. The East Pier at Leith had become a favourite promenade, and 'all that was learned and brilliant in the Edinburgh and Leith society of former days have paced here – Burns and Scott and Carlyle among them', and Hugo Arnot riving at his speldrin and looking, as the Parliament House wit said, "Like his meat"'. This cryptic remark was intended to convey an observed similarity between the skin and bone of Hugo's asthmatic person and a dried haddock he had been eating in the street – a practice not usually associated by future generations with judicial dignity! This learned legal scarecrow combined two notable characteristics of his profession during the eighteenth century – a leaning towards letters and a highly outlandish and individual personality.

Mention the name of Gladstone and every schoolboy will, or until fairly recently certainly would, associate it with one of the great Prime Ministers of Queen Victoria's reign. Although he was brought up and educated in England, he must surely rank, if not as a famous son, at least as a famous grandson of the Port. The family history began in Clydesdale where, according to James Grant, they claimed descent from an 'ancient and not undistinguished stock'. Mr John Gladstones of Toftcombes, near Biggar, in the upper ward of Clydesdale, had by his wife Janet Aitken a son called Thomas who became a prosperous trader in Leith as a flour and barley merchant in the Coal Hill, married Helen, daughter of Mr Walter Neilson of Springfield, and died in 1809. Of that marriage John Gladstone, father of the future statesman, was the eldest son.

John, later Sir John, was born in 1764 in 'the rather gloomy Coal Hill of Leith', and grew up in the area around it and Sheriff Brae. After moving to Liverpool, he acquired a considerable fortune, his Leith apprenticeship standing him in good trading stead, and also became known, through generous gifts of money to the Church of England, as a philanthropist and benefactor. Success having crowned his career in the south, the lure of his native country brought him back to Scotland where he continued his liberality to the Scottish Episcopal Church. He took an active interest in the political controversies of his time, wielding his pen against the repeal of the Corn Laws, and 'desire was more than once expressed to see him in Parliament'. After several unsuccessful attempts, he was elected Conservative Member for Lancaster in 1819. During the years 1821 to 1826 he represented Woodstock, and finally, in 1827, the town of Berwick. On the recommendation of Sir Robert Peel, he was created a baronet in 1846.

Sir John had several children by his second wife, Anne Robertson, daughter of Andrew Robertson, Provost of Dingwall. They called their youngest son William Ewart. Born in 1809, he was destined for greater and more enduring parliamentary fame than that to which his father could lay claim. His father had, nevertheless, risen to the status of a country gentleman with the acquisition of a 'beautiful seat' at Fasque, in the Howe of the Mearns, and it was here that he died on 7th December 1851 aged 86.

William Ewart Gladstone held many offices in Government and was four times Chancellor of the Exchequer. Leaving the Conservative Party to join the Liberals, he became Liberal leader in 1867 and Prime Minister a year later. He retired in 1874 but disagreed so violently with the subsequent Conservative administration's policies that he embarked on his famous Midlothian campaign and set a precedent for politicians of the future by declaiming his election oratory from the rear platform of a Pullman train as he travelled north. As a result of his efforts he was back in office by 1880. The last four years of his life were spent in retirement and the study of theology before his death in 1898. James Grant reminds us that 'Gladstone Place, near the Links, has been so named in honour of this family'.

Another, if perhaps less well remembered, native of the Port was John Home, author of the early Scottish historical play called *Douglas*. In September 1724 he was born in the burgh's Quality Street (now Maritime Street) in a house on the east side and near the northern end, as Grant, always including as much detailed information as he could find, has recorded. His father, Alexander Home, was Town Clerk of Leith and had married Christian, the daughter of an Edinburgh family called Hay. Their son John attended the Kirkgate Grammar School and completed his education at the University of Edinburgh where he studied for the ministry. On his father's side he was descended from Sir James Home of Cowdenknowes who was an ancestor of the Earls of Home. In the present century this family has produced a modern playwright, William Douglas Home, as well as Sir Alec Douglas Home, a recent Prime Minister.

After being licensed by the Edinburgh Presbytery in 1745, John Home temporarily abandoned his chosen profession and joined the corps of volunteers being assembled to confront that most famous Prince of Scottish history who was, in that equally famous year, about to advance on the ancient capital of his forefathers. Charles was on his southern, successful, march and, sweeping on with sanguine prospects, dreamt not yet of his defeat. It was the luckless volunteers who were undone at Falkirk, where Home was captured and cast into custody by the Stuart Army at Doune Castle. But its stone walls did not 'for long a prison make' for the young and energetic John who, along with several other Hanovarian soldiers who had been taken with him, made good their escape by the time-honoured method of tying blankets into ropes and climbing down out of a window. Carrying with them a comrade injured in the descent from their stronghold, they set out for Alloa, where a sloop called the *Vulture* was about the sail for South Queensferry. From there it was a short, safe journey back to Leith and home.

The following year, resuming his clerical vocation, he was called as minister to a church in Athelstaneford where he carried out his pastoral duties for about ten years, and it was during this period that he discovered his talent as a playwright, possibly prompted by the unusual circumstance that his predecessor in the charge, Robert Blair, had been an author. *Agis*, the first of Home's tragedies, was offered in 1749 to the actor David Garrick, who made it clear he was not impressed with it and turned it down, and it was not until 1755 that

185

Douglas, based on an old ballad called 'Gil Morice', was completed. This time he decided to go to London himself and, with the play in his pocket, the divine-turned-dramatist rode south on horseback personally to present his play to Garrick. But Garrick did not think much of *Douglas* either and told the disappointed author he considered it was 'totally unfit for the stage'.

The Rev. John Home now turned his hopes and his attention to a theatrical personality in his native Scotland called West Digges, and the play which was to cause such a storm of controversy and to bring enormous fame to its creator was produced in Edinburgh by Digges in a theatre at the bottom of a close in the Canongate on 14th December 1756, as Robert Chambers noted in his *Traditions*. About two years later it was put on at Covent Garden with Peg Woffington, three years before her death, in the principal female part, and the play continued in unabated popularity for over half a century. In 1950 *Douglas* was performed at the Edinburgh Festival with Dame Sybil Thorndike, over 150 years after the previous production.

Denounced by a Church which saw acting and playwriting by one of its ministers as outrageous, Home decided to resign his charge in East Lothian and devote himself to composing tragedies for the theatre of his day. Deprived of his livelihood, no doubt he was grateful for the annual pension of £300 awarded him by George III, although he was not without some 'sinecure appointments', as Grant calls them, and he was certainly well enough off to be able to support a wife, 'a lady of his own name', whom he married after settling in Edinburgh in 1779. Their 'neat little house' was in North Hanover Street and the actress Mrs Sarah Siddons, when appearing in the City, 'spent an occasional afternoon with Mr and Mrs Home' with whom she usually had an early dinner served by Home's old manservant John.

The playwright counted David Hume, Adam Smith and Dr Alexander Carlyle among his literary friends. He was a captain in the Duke of Buccleuch's Fencibles and never fully recovered from falling from his horse, an accident which took place when he was on parade. This prominent old character of eighteenth-century Edinburgh reached his 84th year notwithstanding, and the seaport claimed him as her own again when he died and was buried on the western side of South Leith Churchyard. A commemorative tablet beside his grave is inscribed 'In memory of John Home, author of the tragedy of "Douglas" etc. Born 13th September 1724. Died 4th September 1808'.

James Grant, however, calls this early example of Scottish dramatic writing 'a rather dull work' which had nevertheless 'maintained a certain popularity', and praises instead a history of the Jacobite Rebellion, 'the task of his declining years', which was published in London in 1802. But it is by *Douglas* that Home has been remembered by all subsequent generations and, as Henry Mackenzie (who preserved many biographical details of his fellow-writer in his Memoirs) is always associated with one book, *The Man of Feeling*, so are John Home and *Douglas* names that are likely to remain inseparable in Scotland's literary annals.

Though by no means a native of Leith, Hugh Miller had several encounters with the Port, but they are of sufficient interest to be given a chapter to themselves.

CHAPTER SEVENTEEN

Hugh Miller and Leith

Hugh Miller, the Cromarty stonemason, eminent geologist, newspaper editor and writer, was born in 1802 in the thatched and whitewashed cottage in Cromarty that has since become a place of pilgrimage and, more recently, a tourist attraction in the North-East of Scotland. This sailor's son who laid bare the mysteries of the Old Red Sandstone in his book, probably his best known work, of that name spent a large part of his life in Edinburgh and related the experiences he had during earlier visits there in his biographical masterpiece, *My Schools and Schoolmasters*.

It was in fact an unusual inheritance that first brought the young Hugh Miller to the south – unusual in that it was an inheritance of which he and his family wanted to rid themselves rather than to possess. The bequest had been to his father and consisted of a ground-floor flat in 'an old brick building four storeys in height', as he later described it, in the Coal Hill in Leith, but as he had died when Hugh was only five years old, nothing could be done about disposing of this vexatious property until Hugh himself, as the son of the beneficiary, had come of age. To begin with, it had provided a small income in rent as it was let as a public house and tap-room, but alterations to the harbour, which resulted in the shipping lying at Coal Hill being brought instead to a lower stretch of the Water of Leith, put an abrupt stop to the business and the rent was reduced by half, the remainder being frequently left unpaid by various 'miserable tenants'.

Mr Veitch, the Town Clerk of Leith and the family's house agent there, wrote 'brief curt letters' that filled Mrs Miller 'with terror and dismay', and the house reached the nadir of its fortunes when it found itself occupied by 'a stout female who kept a certain description of lady lodgers'. On their departure it 'lay untenanted for five years as a result' – untenanted, that is, with the exception of a ghost. The spectre was reported to be that of a 'murdered gentleman whose throat had been cut in an inner apartment by the ladies and his body flung by night into the deep mud of the harbour'. This representation of events in the former tap-room was reduced to its sad if less spectacular reality when one of the ladies themselves was found by the police 'crouching on a lair of straw' and was promptly 'exorcised' into the Bridewell. That being the last that was seen of the ghost, a tenant was found who was not only willing to occupy the property but to pay the rent as well, a state of affairs much too satisfactory to last. The house, not surprisingly, stood in need of essential and costly repair, and another burden was soon to be added as well in the shape of an increase in the parish rates, the heritors having been 'rated for the erection of the magnificent Parish Church of North Leith then in course of building'.

The year was now 1824 and Hugh Miller, having attained competence 'in the eye of the law' to dispose of his unwanted house, determined to lose no time in seeking 'if not a purchaser, at least some one foolish enough to take it off his hands for nothing'. He was also, opportunities to earn his living in the North being few, eager to search for work 'among the stone cutters of Edinburgh' (then considered the most skilled in their particular craft in the world); so there were two pressing reasons for his presence aboard the Leith smack which, four days after leaving Cromarty, was 'threading her way in a morning of light airs and huge broken fog wreaths' through the Firth of Forth. Soon afterwards 'Leith, with its thicket of masts and its tall round tower' lay before him and he came ashore, a strong, powerfully built, muscular figure whose solemn expression probably belied the sense of humour which, as it frequently reveals itself in the pages of My Schools and Schoolmasters, he undoubtedly possessed.

The next day he waited on Mr Veitch, who was able to offer assistance with both undertakings, holding out some hope of a small price for the property and giving him an introduction to a master builder. This was the time of the great building mania in Edinburgh and its environs, and Hugh Miller now found himself, for the ensuing ten months, hewing stones 'under the elm and chestnut trees of Niddrie Park'. A farm servant and his wife in the village took him into their one-roomed cottage, his bed and theirs being on opposite sides with the passage to the door between them. It took him some time to get used to these unaccustomed domestic arrangements. He was even joined, a little later, by a fellow lodger, the goodwife and her husband apparently being in no way put out by such overcrowding and lack of privacy.

This was one of the old eighteenth-century collier villages, now within the boundaries of the City of Edinburgh but then in the country, where the inhabitants had been born into bondage as a consequence of Acts of Parliament which made them the property of the mine owners who employed them, and it took two Acts of Parliament, the second in 1799, to obtain their release from serfdom. Hugh Miller saw it as one of the most singular circumstances of his life that he had conversed with Scotsmen who had been slaves, and the sons of slaves, at the time of their birth only fifty years earlier. Carters and farm labourers made up the rest of the village population and were all, as the stonemason from Cromarty described them, 'ignorant and unintellectual'. Among the colliers, the women bore more marks of serfdom than the men, and theirs had certainly been a hard and soul-destroying life in the pits. They and their children, commonly known as bearers, worked under ground for up to twelve hours a day carrying heavy creels on their backs over long distances from the coal face or, in some mines, ascending ladders till they reached the surface. It was not until 1842 that Lord Shaftsbury with difficulty got a bill through Parliament terminating the engagement of women, and boys under ten years of age, for such employment.

Hugh Miller and his fellow stonemasons were working on additions and improvements at the mansionhouse of Niddrie Marischal, the home of the Wauchopes of Niddrie for eight hundred years. An earlier castle was destroyed in the sixteenth century by an Edinburgh mob because of the 'evil ways' of Archibald Wauchope, the then laird, and although the estate was forfeited and acquired by the Sandilands family, it returned to the Wauchopes in 1608 when the former laird's son made sure of his lost inheritance by marrying a Sandilands daughter. In the seventeenth century John Wauchope of Niddrie was present at the coronation of Charles II, and it was his son who opened new coal workings on his property, paying £54 for sinking a nine-fathom shaft 'at £6 the fathom': £3 went to 'a wife to carrieing the picks too and fra the smiddie' for fifteen days. The price of coal was 2/2d (about 11p) a load. Niddrie Marischal was well known to Lord Cockburn, who wrote in his *Memorials* that he frequently passed Saturdays, Sundays and holidays there for many years.

The last member of this ancient Midlothian family to live in the house was General Andrew Gilbert Wauchope, a compassionate and enlightened man who earned the respect and affectionate loyalty of the Niddrie and New Craighall villagers. He took a keen interest in their welfare, and during the 17-week miners' strike of 1894, when pits were closed throughout the country, he provided his own colliers and their families with food, including vegetables from the Niddrie Marischal garden. The General had been in the Navy during his earlier years and had served with Queen Victoria's son, Prince Alfred, later Duke of Edinburgh. The Prince, when a student at Edinburgh University during the winter of 1863/64 and residing at Holyrood Palace, made several visits to Niddrie where he went pigeon-shooting with his former shipmate. It was General Wauchope's misfortune to have only a brief period of family life. In 1893 he married Jean Muir, daughter of the Principal of the University of Edinburgh, but the war clouds were gathering as the century drew to a close, and he was killed during the Boer War in 1899. Queen Victoria sent a message of sympathy to his widow, who remained at Niddrie Marischal until her death in 1942. The mansionhouse, along with 136 acres of land, was taken over by the Town Council in 1950, and nine years later the house was reduced to an empty shell by a 'spectacular fire', as an Edinburgh newspaper described it at the time. General Wauchope's biographer, William Baird, makes reference to the young stonemason from Cromarty who was employed at Niddrie House in 1824 and who was traditionally believed to have been responsible for the carving of some ornamental chimneys in the mansion.

During his period at Niddrie, Hugh Miller made frequent expeditions to Edinburgh to acquaint himself with the City, climbing Arthur's Seat to watch the sun go down behind the Lomond Hills in Fife, and gaining the same pleasure from the antique aspects of the town as he got from the wild and picturesque countryside with which he was more familiar in the north. He felt that he had seen 'not one, but two cities – a city of the past and a city of the present – set down side by side, as if for purposes of comparison'.

It was not long before he discovered among some of his fellow workmen at Niddrie a predilection for the theatrical entertainments which could be enjoyed in the capital. A seat in the gallery of the Theatre Royal, in Shakespeare Square, cost 1/- [5p], and the stonemasons were usually willing to sacrifice that sum from their wages at the end of the week. Hugh was not so enthusiastic as some of the others, but he made occasional visits to the old theatre in their company. One of them in particular, identified only as 'Davie' and who lodged in another cottage, was a 'wayward, eccentric lad and stage mad'. This rustic devotee of the boards had even written a play himself. Young Miller considered that, for the stage, 'nature had fitted him rather indifferently', it being his misfortune to have 'a squat, ungainly figure, an inexpressive face and a voice that . . . somewhat resembled . . . a carpenter's saw'.

A spectacle of a very different order brought Hugh and his friends hot foot to the City on another occasion. In November 1824 the Great Fire of Edinburgh broke out in the High Street and Parliament Square and raged unabated for several days. News of the conflagration, in which 400 families were rendered homeless, was soon carried to Niddrie, with the prediction that the masons could now look forward to rebuilding the Old Town in its entirety; so they set off that night to witness the fiery destruction that might give them so much employment in the future.

However restricted and, as he himself considered it until he grew more accustomed to it, unseemly his village lodgings may have been, they were presumably to be preferred to the unsavoury slum in Leith of which he was endeavouring to rid himself, and in order to do so he had to keep company on the occasions when he visited it with a character then notorious in the Port called Peter McCraw who appears to have been as unprepossessing as the property. McCraw was a house agent, a man with only one hand and an unenviable reputation for pitiless persistence in his other capacity, that of tax collector. The place was being used as sleeping quarters by tramps, and a heap of straw in one of the corners indicated the presence of one such unwanted tenant. 'Ah! said McCraw, 'got in again, I see. The shutters must be looked to.' Other things required looking to as well. The walls were blackened by smoke, plaster had fallen, or was still hanging, from the ceiling, and the bars of the grates had rusted till they were as 'red as foxtails'. The stonemason attempted a humorous approach. 'Its terrible to be married for life to a baggage of a house like this and made liable, like other husbands, for all its debts,' he said. 'Is there no way of getting a divorce?' But the house agent was not to be drawn and answered emphatically that he didn't know.

Years afterwards Hugh Miller was surprised to encounter Peter McCraw in a poem, or song, as he expressed it, by 'poor Gilfillan', none other than the Poet of Leith himself, called

'The Tax-Gatherer'. Gilfillan showed little sympathy for his subject in lines that reveal the extent to which McCraw was feared and hated by the local population:

> There's hope o' a ship though she's sair pressed with dangers,
>   An' roun' her frail timmers the angry winds blaw;
> I've aften gat kindness unlooked for frae strangers,
>   But wha need hope kindness frae Peter McCraw?
> I've kent a man pardoned when just at the gallows —
>   I've kent a chiel honest whose trade was the law!
> I've kent fortune's smile even fa' on gude fellows;
>   But I ne'er kent exception wi' Peter McCraw!

The following year Hugh Miller got himself 'as surely dissevered from the Coal-hill as paper and parchment could do it', but the next time he passed 'his umquhile house' it was derelict and boarded up.

After falling a victim to 'stonecutter's malady', caused by the penetration of his lungs by stone dust, he returned to Cromarty where, in the fresh sea air of the North-East coast, the condition improved. He now felt, however, that a change of occupation was essential, not only for the sake of his health but also because his active mind required more intellectual stimulation than could be obtained from the hewing of stones. This led him first to employment in a bank after his marriage to Lydia Fraser, also of Cromarty, but an opportunity to embark on the work for which he was outstandingly suited came in 1839 when he was asked by the Evangelical Party to become the first editor of the Free Church newspaper they were about to launch called *The Witness*. This appointment brought him back to Edinburgh, and the family settled at 16 Archibald Place. (Hugh Miller is prominently portrayed by D. O. Hill in his famous 'Disruption' painting in the Free Church Offices on the Mound.)

The geological articles which were later published collectively under the title of *The Old Red Sandstone* appeared originally in *The Witness*, but he became increasingly interested in, and later obsessively influenced by, the theological controversy which above all others at that time was exercising the minds and conscience of churchmen. The discoveries of Charles Darwin were opening new and disturbing avenues of evolutionary thought, and it was to be many years before Christian thinking would be able to recognise that theology and science were mutually complementary rather than mutually exclusive.

It was in a house called Shrub Mount, beside St. Mark's Church in Portobello, that Hugh Miller spent the last years of his life with his wife and children. Here he created a museum of geology, the study of which, together, later, with theology, had been the principal concern and overriding interest of his life. The adverse effects of mental stress were now becoming apparent in the mind of this 'physical giant', as Sydney Dobell, to whom 'he complained much of his broken health', was to write. He began to have irrational doubts about the safety of his geological collection and even of his own life, and took to sleeping with firearms beside him during the night. In an attempt to answer his critics and to clarify his own fevered thinking on the scientific implications of his discoveries among the fossil-bearing stones that told their own silent but irrefutable story to their investigators, he commenced *The Testimony of the Rocks*, a book destined never to be finished. In 1856, at the age of only 54, he wrote a farewell letter to his wife and put an end to his mental anguish with a revolver.

'His funeral', as James Grant has written, 'was a vast and solemn one.' It was winter, and thawing snow covered the streets, but this did not deter the Edinburgh crowds who came in 'thick masses' to watch in respectful silence the passing of the cavalcade to the Grange Cemetery. Even the shops were closed as the whole town mourned an outstanding Scotsman. Another name in the City's literary galaxy had entered into history, and there was a fine appropriateness in the placing of his grave, for he lies next to Thomas Nelson, one of her greatest publishers.

How many people in the course of a lifetime encounter

genius unaware? Among the thick masses in the Portobello streets could there have been some who had hewn stones under the shade of Niddrie Woods some thirty years before? Did the squat, ungainly, stage-struck Davie, or even the callous, one-armed Peter McCraw, if he still survived to wreak injustice in the port of Leith, casting back their minds to see again the stalwart figure of the young stonemason from the Cromarty cottage, salute his memory as he passed on his last untimely journey?

He had paid the price of that rare possession, a mind moulded to pioneer on the edges of human understanding and discovery and, by so doing, had carved out a path for others who were to follow him and, like the rocks themselves, had left his own particular testimony, for there is nothing hidden that shall not ultimately be revealed.

CHAPTER EIGHTEEN

The New Haven

While in the Second half of the twentieth century cities expand into sprawling, concrete conurbations and new towns spring up to meet industrial demand in a time of rapid social and scientific change, many of the old centres of maritime trade, commerce and population have subsided into quiet, forgotten backwaters visited only by the painstaking researcher of the past or, where organised publicity has placed them on the tourist tracks, the casual observer and the curious. But this sequence of events is far from being a recent one. It has in fact been taking place, usually on a much more gradual scale, throughout the history of man's relationship with his environment.

An example of this flowing and ebbing tide in the geographical significance of towns and villages is the little hamlet of Blackness on the Firth of Forth. Once the thriving port of the inland town of Linlithgow three miles to the south-west, with its ancient castle guarding the upper reaches of the Forth, it lost its status in proportion as the old trading patterns changed and increased shipping tonnage restricted cargo-carrying vessels to the deeper water of the Forth estuary. It was known as the Haven and when, in 1493, King James IV obtained from Abbot Ballantyne of Holyrood the coastal part of the extensive barony of Broughton for the purpose of dock and harbour building, he saw to it that houses and a rope-walk were provided in addition, and his choice of name for the location of this development was New Haven to distinguish it from the old one. Blackness was a place of some standing at the time when it was customary for Scotland's kings to make frequent use of their Palace at Linlithgow; and when the Regent Moray, during the minority of James VI, was assassinated in the town in 1570, his body was taken to Blackness. From there it was conveyed by sea to Leith where it lay in the church now known as South Leith prior to burial within St. Giles in Edinburgh.

The New Haven was also known as Our Lady's Port of Grace on account of a chapel dedicated to the Virgin there, the roofless outside walls of which can still be seen today. The chapel was later dedicated to St. James as well and appears to have been a daughter church of St. Anthony's Preceptory in Leith, as Grant records that 'in 1614, with its grounds, it was

Newhaven, a fishing village by the Forth in which very few of its original buildings now survive.

198

conveyed in the same charter to the Kirk Session of South
Leith by James VI'. As early as 1511 James had granted
Newhaven to the Burgesses of Edinburgh, and the superiority was in fact the first of their voracious acquisitions which
later encompassed nearly the whole of Leith.

It was here that the famous Forth-built warship, the *Great
Michael*, was constructed by the fourth James, who was satisfied
that in it he possessed the world's finest ocean-going vessel,
which had solid oak amidships as much as ten feet thick and
was launched in 1511, a year no doubt well remembered by
those who witnessed it. But the ship had a short and undistinguished life. Her instructions, which were to proceed to
France, would seem to have been disobeyed, as she is next
heard of, in the few and rather unreliable surviving records,
as bearing down on the Irish coast in a plundering raid! After
the untimely death of the King at Flodden Field, the *Michael*
was sold to Louis XII, and she was later reported to have been
'suffered to rot in the harbour of Brest', a sad end for such a
noble craft. James IV did not live to bring his plans for a
Scottish Navy to fruition. It has been said that he hoped to
outstrip the port of Leith with his carefully designed and up-
to-date New Haven, but if so, that popular but unfortunate
monarch was not destined to come within sight of achieving
that ambition either.

As might be expected, Edinburgh owned the Newhaven
oyster fishings and, ceremonial being dear to the heart of all
burgesses, an annual 'stately progress' to the Port was made
for the purpose of assessing the quality and quantity of these
highly marketable delicacies and of 'rouping' the fishings.
They even took to the boats and 'solemnly cruised' above the
oyster beds maturing profitably beneath the Firth. During
the later 1700s the popularity of oysters was at its height, and
high society as well as low spent long hours in the taverns
and oyster cellars of the City where 'raw oysters and flagons
of porter were set out plentifully on a table in a dingy wain-
scoted room lighted by tallow candles'. They were in such

demand that the 'home-grown' variety had to be augmented by others imported frequently from Holland. Such inroads, in fact, were being made into the oyster population, and so many seedling oysters taken from the water and sold to foreign buyers for the creation of new oyster beds in other countries, that steps were taken to prevent over-dredging. In 1790 an imaginative method of conservation was attempted. Brass and iron 'patterns' were manufactured and distributed to the Newhaven fishermen, specimens being kept in Leith also at the Shore Dues Office; anyone found selling oysters smaller than the size of the pattern was fined and the overseas sale of oysters was banned completely. Beds were also situated at the Black Rocks near Leith Harbour and at Inchkeith, and

Surviving buildings in Newhaven Village.

disputes with Prestonpans over the right to these oyster fishings were not uncommon. Dredging, however, was often carried on under cover of darkness and went undetected. Eventually all efforts to save the oyster scalps of the Forth proved unavailing. In fairness to the Newhaven fishermen it has to be said that the principal damage was done by outsiders who rented the scalps and brought in their own dredging vessels; even the Duke of Buccleuch, who owned some of the oyster beds, was interested only in profit and could not be persuaded to introduce conservation measures. Restocking was contemplated as late as 1897, but long before that the day of the lucrative but abused oyster fishings was at an end.

The old tradition that oysters should only be eaten when there is an 'R' in the month corresponds exactly with the oyster season which starts at the beginning of September and continues to the end of April. The mussels gathered along the coastline were also a regular source of revenue in the Newhaven Fishmarket until as recently as 1955. In that year the shellfish beds were found to be contaminated, and the trade in mussels followed that of the oysters into oblivion.

The Newhaven oyster-women's was one of the best-known and most beautiful of the old street cries of Edinburgh, all now as much a part of history as the traditional costume of the fisherwomen themselves, and their closes and forestaired houses in the village have disappeared as well. At the top of Whale Brae, now the lower part of Newhaven Road, stood Admiralty House (demolished in the 1930s) beside the Fishermen's Park where the nets were set out to dry, and where some of the fishing yawls were built and repaired in a former sailmaker's shed. The Park was taken over by the city in 1920, that fateful year for the whole of Leith, and only a small part of it remains today. Further up Newhaven Road, beside Victoria Park, stands the much-altered Victoria Park House, built in 1789 and originally known as Bonnington Park House. Bought by Edinburgh Town Council in 1918, it was here, during the smallpox epidemic of 1942, that persons thought liable to contract the disease through having been in contact with it were isolated for a period of twenty-one days. After the epidemic the building returned to its former use of housing a day nursery for children in which capacity it has served the community for many years.

From the seventeenth century, if not earlier, the services of pilot boats, owned and supervised by a pilot master, were available at Leith and Newhaven where exceptional skill in navigation often bridged the gap between seawreck and survival among the submerged rocks of the Forth in treacherous winter weather. On land, the Newhaven stagecoach, in the early years of the nineteenth century, carried the fishwives and other passengers from the village to the Tron Church and back three times a day, a distance, as the gull flies, of just over two miles.

During the middle years of the nineteenth century the regular loading of gunpowder on to Government ships at Newhaven was, not surprisingly, a source of concern to the residents of the village itself and of neighbouring Trinity. The danger was greatly increased by the casual behaviour of the seamen handling the lethal barrels, who smoked their pipes, in spite of fines and reprimands, while so employed. As happens in any age when adverse local opinion has been roused, a public meeting was held to consider what should be done, and an appeal was immediately sent to the Home Secretary in London. The appeal proved effective, and in 1874 the shipment of gunpowder was removed to Leith.

In the Peacock Hotel, always famed for its fish, Newhaven has had for many years a picturesque link with its past both architecturally and gastronomically. Peacock was the name of the original owner, and in a recent restoration an old fireplace decorated with a well-preserved peacock in coloured tiles was discovered, as well as a group of three stained-glass windows which had been boarded up. Another building, the Newhaven Free Fishermen's Hall built in 1877, was reconstructed some years ago along with adjoining property to form new premises for a motor boat club, the interior being remodelled to resemble that of King James IV's Newhaven-built warship, the *Great Michael*.

The men of Newhaven have been noted for their courage both in peace and war. In January 1816 a Scandinavian vessel, in danger of foundering off Inchkeith, flew a distress signal from her masthead which was sighted by the Newhaven pilots. Nine of them set out to the rescue in heavy seas about ten o'clock in the morning and succeeded by strenuous effort in getting three men on board. They were only just in time, as the master was ordering the masts to be cut down. Thanks to their expert seamanship and local knowledge the narrow

One of the last remaining closes in Newhaven in 1972.

203

waters between rocks to the south of the island were safely negotiated, and the vessel was able to reach the shelter of Elie harbour without misadventure, the captain gratefully paying the one hundred guineas charged by the Newhaven pilots whose lives had been in danger throughout. At the beginning of the nineteenth century the fee was three guineas (£3.15p) for normal pilotage from the May Island into Leith roads for ships of 150 tons and over, but only £2:12:6 (£2.63p) if the vessel was 'two leagues above the May'.

The fishermen of Newhaven won praise for their conspicuous patriotism during the war with France, when they formed themselves into a marine defence force to guard the coastline. In recognition of this service a silver medal was presented to the Newhaven Free Fishermen's Society in 1796 and was worn by the Society's boxmaster every year during their procession through Leith, Edinburgh, Granton and Trinity. Unfortunately a letter signed by George III 'expressing his satisfaction at their loyalty' was lost after being preserved by the Society for many years.

During the 1860s the Town Council of Leith would appear to have been experiencing difficulty in keeping the streets of Newhaven in good order, as a number of prosecutions are recorded in the *Leith Burghs Pilot*. These consisted principally of the throwing of rubbish in the shape of cabbage leaves and potato peelings on to the roads and pavements, and for this offence a fine of about half a crown (13p) with the option of four days' imprisonment was usually imposed. Some boys, who would persist in being boys, were severely warned and admonished for stealing apples and causing damage to private gardens, and then dismissed, in 1864. The commonest offences were drunkenness and disorderly behaviour and the stealing of coal, but in 1881 two women were jailed for ten days after taking three cotton sheets and a linen apron from a clothes line on the public thoroughfare in Darling's Close in Leith – a nineteenth-century version of shoplifting! Petty crimes and the names of their perpetrators were the stuff of local news reporting, along with verbatim reports of deliberations in the Leith Town Council Chamber, and a surprising and comprehensive coverage of foreign news. Devoid, of course, of photographs, but presenting column after extensive column of well-printed, well-written and, in accordance with the higher if more pedantic literary standards of the time, meticulously expressed information on current affairs and prevailing public opinion, the *Leith Burghs Pilot* circulated through Leith, Portobello, Dalkeith, Newhaven, Granton and Cramond and was beyond doubt excellent value at one old penny. An editorial note in one edition is indicative of the manners that maketh man in any period of history but would never, like so much else, find a place among present-day journalese: 'We shall be willing at all times to throw our

Newhaven Harbour and Lighthouse, once the colourful scene of the still famous fishwives in their traditional costume.

columns open to correspondents who write in a gentlemanly and courteous spirit, whatever their views might be; and shall give correspondents of diametrically opposite opinions an impartial hearing.'

Of the old historic fishing village, there is not much to be encountered on the ground today. Late twentieth-century housing casting a few backward glances at tradition cannot perpetuate the distinctive personality of the original New Haven and, unlike its predecessor Blackness, there is no ancient fortress around which to concentrate an imaginative recreation of its significant years. To attempt this, the harbour is probably the most promising place, with its colourful fleet of little boats and the white lighthouse on the seawall lifting its eye unto the Firth. The creels and petticoats of the fisher lassies are to be seen there no more and, like the oysters and the inimitable street cries of their vendors, are not likely to return.

CHAPTER NINETEEN

History from an Early Newspaper

The date is Saturday, February 28th 1807, two years after Trafalgar and eight years before Waterloo in the reign of George III; the title *The Caladonian Mercury*; the printer Robert Allan at the Old Fishmarket Close in Edinburgh; and the price sixpence (3p).

The reason for the survival for nearly two hundred years of a four-page, closely printed newspaper, in which references to Leith are numerous, in the family of the original owner is not now known, but a keen interest in (and an awareness of the historic nature of the outcome of) the bitter controversy then occupying the minds and printing presses of the period surrounding the brutal and all too financially profitable slave trade is certainly a possible explanation. It was in that eventful year of 1807 that Britain finally abolished that barbarous practice in its colonial empire, and under the proud heading of 'Imperial Parliament' the last passionate debate in the House of Commons, and the passing of the Bill by an overwhelming majority, can still be deciphered in the minutely printed columns of this brittle, faded forerunner of the mass media, where it is presented as it took place without comment or criticism; and also without illustration, as photography was still as unknown as wireless or the internal combustion engine.

After so momentous an event the daily mundanities of the time seem anti-climactic by comparison, but are also of interest in their own right as a microcosm of local social history at the beginning of a century which, as we move towards the year 2000, is becoming increasingly remote.

The intermittent Napoleonic Wars were in progress and, Leith not yet having been superseded by the Clyde as Scotland's most important arrival and departure point for merchant shipping, there are several announcements of loading dates for vessels 'armed by Government' against enemy interception on the high seas. 'At Leith for London', reads one such advertisement, 'The Old Shipping Co.'s Smack Caledonia, Robt. Nisbet Master, will take goods till Tuesday morning at nine o'clock.' 'The John is a new vessel, about 300 tons burden, and sails fast', says another, with the information that she will leave for Halifax and Prince Edward Island on 20th March. Also 'at Leith taking in goods for London direct' is the 'Union Shipping Company's Smack, armed with six 18-pound carronades, Eliza, Mark Sanderson Master', which will sail on Tuesday morning at 8 o'clock. The Sloop *Hope* was anchored at Leith as well, waiting to receive goods on board for Shetland, and would sail on 6th March.

Victuallers and provision merchants advertise their wares without recourse to sales promotion tricks or stratagems. James Reid of the Luckenbooths can supply his customers with 'new Pickled Herrings, of an excellent quality, just arrived from the West Highlands in Barrels, Firkins and Half Firkins' along with 'Aberdeen pickled cod in Small Kitts for the convenience of private families', as well as 'Virgin Honey in Jars of one and two pints each'. 'Tickets for a Lottery' makes surprising reading. These could be obtained at the Licensed Office of Dan Forrest opposite the Tron Church. In the two preceding Lotteries capital prizes of £20,000 and £500 had been sold in shares, which would seem to indicate that gambling was as popular and profitable in the Edinburgh of the early nineteenth century as honey and salted fish.

The timber trade was also flourishing and, imported from the Baltic, wood destined for panelling and furniture had been unloaded regularly on the quays at Leith for at least two hundred years. 'To be peremptorily sold at auction', states one announcement succinctly, 'in Martin's Coal Yard, Constitution

Street, Leith, on Mon. 2 March at 12 o'clock, 700 Christiana Red Wood Deals 10-12 feet in length . . . and 300 Gottenburg Deals.' A police force was in the early stages of its development in the Port, and an advertisement for a suitable person to take charge was inserted with a commendable economy of words: 'Wanted for the towns of South and North Leith, Citadel, Coal Hill, Territory of St. Anthony and Yardheads an Intendent of Police'. And another item not likely to be read in any newspaper of the present day concerned 'deserters from His Majesty's 43 (or Argyllshire) Regiment of British Militia' and listed eleven names with detailed descriptions of the men involved.

In spite of war and rumours of invasion, social activities continued without interruption, and the paper gives due space to the current entertainments.

The sixth and last subscription concert of the season at Corrie's Rooms was to be followed, as usual, by a Grand Ball – 'admission to non-subscribers 5/-' (25p). Mr N. Corrie is listed in the Edinburgh Post Office Directory for 1807 as a music seller with Concert Rooms in Leith Walk. He begged leave 'to return his warmest thanks to the subscribers for the present season, and to express his hopes that they intend continuing their subscriptions' for the next, for which subscription books 'were now open at Mr Corrie's music shop'. And if these pleasurable distractions were not enough to raise the spectators' spirits and banish their fears, they could always have recourse to Dr Innes' Compound Strengthening Powders, obtainable in sealed parcels, price 6/– (30p) including duty, from 'Mr Manderson, apothecary, in Rose Street'. Their salutary effects in restoring 'the weak, debilitated and nervous constitutions of the young and old of both sexes to health and vigour', while not guaranteed, were clearly considered to be beyond reasonable dispute.

Another announcement concerning Leith is interesting in that it reflects the longstanding antagonism between the City and its Port: 'A notice having appeared in this paper, addressed to the inhabitants of Leith, calculated to induce a belief that the Magistrates and Council of this city had relinquished altogether a plan they have in view for certain improvements at the west end of Leith Links, we are authorised to state that this is by no means the case, and that the plan has been given up for the present, not in consequence of any intimation, as erroneously stated in the anonymous notice, but with a view of accelerating the passing of an Act of Parliament, the leading purposes of which are totally different and unconnected with Leith Links, of which the Magistrates and Council, as representing the community of Edinburgh, are proprietors'.

The advertisements dealing with property for sale and to let are presented in a picturesque linguistic style: 'That house in Clamshell Turnpike entering from the High Street' (Edinburgh – Old Town) 'which may, at a trifling expense, be converted into two', can be seen 'every lawful day from 1 to 3'. By order of the Lord Provost and Magistrates several building lots are offered for sale – the remaining areas, on the west and east ends of London Street on the north side, and one or two gap sites as yet unbuilt on in Charlotte Square together with stable ground behind (Edinburgh – New Town which in 1807 was still in course of building). A house in Nicolson Street 'lately possessed by the Honourable Miss Grey, above Mr Core's china shop' is to be rouped on the 6th of March. 'Three sides of a square, to be called Hermitage Square, measuring upwards of six acres English, part of the lands of Hermitage' are to be feued for building. This desirable residential site is 'within five minutes' walk of Leith, and ten minutes' walk of the sea-beach, where machines for bathing can be had at all hours'. It might well be wondered whether the opportunity for a midnight dip would be attractive to potential buyers on the east-windswept east coast, but its convenient situation for recreations more suited to the climate might have been considered favourable. Bounded on the north by the lands belonging to Lady Fife, the ground commanded a most extensive view of the Firth of Forth, the City of Edinburgh, the town of Leith and the adjacent country, and lay 'two or three hundred yards from the Golf-house of Leith, entering by the road from Leith to Lochend'.

No. 3 St. James's Place, Leith, 'being in a pleasant, healthy situation' on the north side of the road leading to Jock's Lodge, is on offer, along with the large and commodious house called Bonnington Lodge 'situate on the road to Newhaven' with a hay-loft and stable with two stalls suitable for 'a large and genteel family'. Details of extensive accommodation are given for several of the houses in this section, including such features – unlikely to sharpen their competitive selling edge for future generations – as garrets, closets, coal- and wash-houses, cellars, catacombs (as those cold and dark old dungeons with recesses or pigeon-holes for the storage of wine were called) and water-pumps which were needed to get the water, now available by dint of primitive plumbing in individual houses, above the level of the basement.

The notice that 'On Wednesday the 2nd batallion of the 42nd regiment, or Royal Highlanders, marched through this city for Leith, where they are to embark for Fort George', brings us back to the War and the coastline defences against a possible French invasion; and the reported death of Mr William Simpson, a papermaker at Lasswade, takes us back to a still earlier war in the reign of George III, as Mr Simpson 'had served under Lord Cornwallis, as an officer of artillery, during the American War'.

It is doubtful if newspapers of the late twentieth century, even allowing for photographs, banner headlines and two-page-spread advertisements, offer their readers more balanced, impartial, varied and well-presented news in the much greater space at their disposal than is contained in the four faded and fascinating pages of this once-folded single sheet. Every effort had been made to include the latest and most accurate reports, without benefit of telephone or radio, from the theatres of war, and the account of Parliamentary proceedings is ingrained with the natural assumption that Great Britain deserved its name and would never lose its greatness or its power. The triumph of terminating the odious traffic in human lives was all the greater for having been accomplished by a nation at war and, as G. M. Trevelyan was to write over a century later. 'If Wilberforce could convert England, she would soon persuade the world'. And in 1807 that was exactly what she did.

CHAPTER TWENTY

Houses by the Forth

There are many reasons why people put down roots, but in bygone times they tended to be closely linked with the potential of particular areas to provide the basic environmental requirements for survival and their possible subsequent development for future prosperity. It was in such favourable places that families became established, sometimes for generation after generation, passing on what they had achieved to be built on and expanded by their successors, and it is this process of land selection that explains the numbers of old and interesting houses in distinctive groupings in different parts of the country. Fertile soil for food production and coastal belts and natural harbours for fishing and trading are natural locations in which a rich heritage of vernacular tradition and its attendant architecture are principally to be found. In varying degrees all these features were there for the exploiting around the shores of Forth, and it is therefore not surprising that such houses as have fortunately survived, in whole or in part, to the present day should be full of local, and sometimes national, history and general interest.

Furthest to the east, and situated at the edge of the coalmining district that stretches across to Musselburgh, is Brunstane House, approached across a bridge which is itself of interest because of age but, dating in fact from the eighteenth century, is not as old as tradition, which harks it back to the Romans, would suggest. Originally known as Gilbertoun, the house belonged in the early years of the sixteenth century to John Crichton, who gave it the name of Brunstane after his castle near Penicuik. Alexander Crichton, his son, was

213

involved in the murder of Cardinal Beaton, and the building was pulled down in consequence. John Geddie describes how, in 1593, the lands were alienated to 'Dame Jane Fleming, Lady Thirlestane, the widow of Chancellor Maitland', and her son, the first Earl of Lauderdale, entered into possession of them. His more famous son, John Maitland, afterwards Duke of Lauderdale, succeeded to them, and his arms, together with those of his first wife, were carved over the entrance, beside the date 1639, when he had completed the rebuilding of the mansion. About thirty years later the Duke, strong, unscrupulous, a member of the notorious Cabal of Charles II, and a mighty wielder of unopposed power in Scotland, greatly strengthened the historic interest of Brunstane by employing the King's Architect in Scotland, Sir William Bruce, to enlarge the house. The Duchess having died in January 1671, Lauderdale embarked upon his second marriage the following month to the probably disreputable and certainly scheming and determined Countess of Dysart. She was also the cousin of her new husband's architect, and it is worth noting that Sir William Bruce's second wife spent her widowhood in the demilitarised Citadel in Leith after his death.

Brunstane House was enlarged by Bruce in much the same way as he extended Holyrood Palace for Charles II. A projecting corner tower was built to correspond with the older tower already in existence, and both structures were then linked by a symmetrical central range containing the entrance. Perhaps the most interesting apartment in the house is the octagonal dining-room, 'wainscotted and ceilinged', says John Geddie, 'in dark oak, with elaborately ornamented chimneypiece, bearing the royal and the Lauderdale arms, and with panel-paintings (of which there are over seventy in the house) – the scene of much wassailing and of good, or more often evil, counselling in the most troubled time in the history of the Scottish Church and State'. The building contains some of the earliest sash windows in the country.

After the Lauderdales, Burnstane passed to the Duke of

Brunstane House, the Edinburgh home of the notorious
Earl of Lauderdale during the reign of Charles II.

Argyle and in 1747, together with part of the estate, to Andrew
Fletcher of Saltoun (a nephew of the great champion of
Scotland's independence of the same name) who, as Lord
Milton, became Lord Justice-Clerk at the time of the '45 and
who died there in 1766. Three years later it was bought by the
eighth Earl of Abercorn, who already owned the remaining
lands through their having been purchased by the third Earl
from the Duke of Argyle, and his descendant, the first Duke
of Abercorn, sold the house to the Benhar Coal Company in
1875. With extensive alterations by William Adam for Lord
Milton and plasterwork of exceptional merit, the house,

215

which is still in occupation, retains much of its former splendour and is a building of both local and national importance.

Brunstane stands well back from the sea, behind the streets of Joppa and the Brunstane Burn that runs beneath the 'Roman' bridge, and the attractively composed walls and turrets of Craigentinny House are also some distance from the water. In the old vernacular style with extensions of the seventeenth and nineteenth centuries, it was the home of the Nisbets of Dean and Craigentinny and, latterly, of the Millers, a merchant family whose eldest sons were always called William. The house and surrounding lands were acquired by William Miller, a Quaker seed merchant from Holyrood Road, when the Nisbets died out in 1764. John Russell calls the house the most interesting of the mansions of Restalrig. In 1780, so tradition has it, the laird, being in his 91st year, considered the time had come to ensure the succession to yet another of his name, and installed in his house a bride said to be rather less than forty years his junior. The idea of settling down immediately did not apparently appeal, and they embarked on an odyssey of European travel. When news reached his tenants that another William had been born in Paris – his mother being in fact 42 – they inclined towards a degree of scepticism, but the nonagenarian parent and his wife returned, and the child was brought up at Craigentinny where in due course he inherited the estate.

Not surprisingly, the last of the William Millers, though becoming a public figure and Member of Parliament for an English constituency, was an eccentric character, not the least of his oddities being the instructions contained in his will, presumably intended to discourage the curious from digging up his remains to discover the secret of his peculiarities. The directions were observed to the letter when he was buried on his own estate, a short distance from the Portobello Road, beneath forty feet of earth and with a large, elaborate monument on top. Known as the Craigentinny Marbles and completed in 1856, the Monument caused widespread interest at the time and can still be seen among the surrounding streets and beyond the grey stone walls of the old farmhouse of Wheatfield. Built in the style of a diminutive Greek temple, it replicates a tomb on the Appian Way in Rome and was designed by the Edinburgh architect, David Rhind. The sculptured panels depicting the overthrow of Pharaoh in the Red Sea and the Song of Miriam and Moses were the work of Alfred Gatley.

There have been other houses of distinction in this area, and one which has survived among the modern complexities of Leith housing developments and has in recent years been

The Craigentinny Marbles; a diminutive Greek temple, it marks the grave of the eccentric William Miller beside the Portobello Road.

rediscovered is the Regency villa at Seafield called Seacote House. It is now a B-listed building and dates from around 1820 but in 1985 stood in need of some attention and repair. About ten years ago a plan was agreed to convert it into two flats, with the grounds providing space for new houses within a landscaped development project, on similar lines to those carried out at Easter Park, an interesting 'reproduction' house at Barnton, and also overlooking the sea across a golf course, built in the Adam manner in 1905 by a family well known in the tea trade called Melrose and last owned by the Younger family who sold it with its grounds to a developer. In the Autumn of 1983, however, events took a different turn when a construction company applied for permission to demolish Seacote and build six dwellinghouses on the site. This application was fortunately unsuccessful, and the survival of the house is no longer threatened.

Drylaw, another historic house away to the west, is also well distanced from the Firth. Unseen from outside, it hides among green lawns and fruit trees and behind old weathered walls and was originally built in 1718. Like many others, this early Georgian house was turned back to front when reconstructed in the 1780s, and the short flight of steps with curving iron handrails on the other side of the building marks the former entrance. The ashlar facade added at the later date to the new frontage displays all the distinguishing features – columned portico, semicircular fanlight and central pediment – of the new and developing style. Inside are small pine-panelled rooms and a brass-finialed, wrought-iron stair recalling the slightly earlier one, mentioned later, at Caroline Park. Too late to be a Bruce house and too early even for William Adam, famous father of more famous sons, its original rubble walls and harling, its layout and conception generally make Drylaw a typical and wholly satisfying Scottish house of its period and an exemplary manifestation of indigenous culture absorbing and subsuming outside influences to create a recognisable national idiom. Although it is known that the Loch

family, who built the house, were on terms of personal friend-
ship with the Adams, there is no documentary evidence to
support the suggestion that they were involved in designing it.
The house has so far managed to survive but redevelopment
has overtaken the grounds in which it stands. Nearby, the
original Drylaw Mains farmhouse does duty as a police station
on Ferry Road.

In 1683 Sir George Mackenzie, Viscount Tarbat, bought the
lands of Royston with which went Granton Castle, a ruined
keep on the estate, and the substantial mid-16th century
Royston House, a building very much in the Scottish vernac-

Drylaw House, a beautiful 18th century mansion now redeveloped
to meet 20th century requirements.

ular tradition with a re-entrant stair tower, probably erected after Hertford's invasion of 1544. In 1684 work commenced on the reconstruction and extension of Royston House around a quadrangle, and it is this enlarged building which Mackenzie called a 'cottage' in an inscription above the entrance lintel (probably in much the same spirit as George IV when Prince Regent referred to his architect Nash's Royal Lodge at Windsor as a 'cottage' about 130 years later). In 1739 Royston House was bought by 'John, the "Great Duke of Argyle and Greenwich"' who figures prominently in Scott's *Heart of Midlothian*, as noted by John Geddie, and who renamed it Caroline Park 'in compliment to the consort of George II'. His daughter married Lord Dalkeith, later Duke of Buccleuch, which circumstance took Caroline Park into Buccleuch ownership.

This ducal mansionhouse has an ironwork balcony above a projecting portico between two ogival-roofed towers and outstanding ornaments of the interior are the magnificent wrought-iron stair already mentioned and painted panels on the walls and ceilings.

Two tales of the supernatural, their origins no doubt deep in the ravelled history of its past, still cling to Caroline Park. One is of a ghostly cannoball which was seen from time to time to bounce in the drawing-room without causing injury or damage, and the other is of a green lady who rises at midnight from a moss-covered well to ring a bell in the courtyard. Whether relevant to such lore or not, human remains have been found in the vicinity. During excavations graves were discovered containing bones which may have been those of a ship's crew which landed at Granton in the 17th century. They had died of plague and were known to have been buried near the house.

In more recent times this gnarled but splendidly surviving mansion became flanked by somewhat unseemly neighbours – on the west by Granton Gasworks and by an oil depot on the east. It was for many years the Factory and Chemical Works

The mansionhouse of Caroline Park, an imposing ducal residence
in a deteriorated environment.

of A. B. Fleming & Co. Ltd., who operated in London,
Capetown and Melbourne, had branches in Birmingham,
Liverpool, Dundee and Glasgow and who claimed to be the
'largest printing ink factory in the world'. During this time, to
the great credit of Fleming & Co., care was constantly taken
to preserve the fabric of the building. After their departure to
larger premises, occupations of short duration followed and
in 1979 it was leased by The Buccleuch Estates Ltd, for use as
office accommodation. Now however the wheel has come full
circle and the mansionhouse (which was at one time the home
of Lady John Scott, the author and composer of *Annie Lawrie*)
is once again a family home.

Granton Castle disappeared very gradually from the scene, the last fragments being swept away within the last twenty years.

Not far away the grounds of the former Granton House, to the east of the present-day West Shore Road, have been completely swallowed up by the massive Scottish Gas complex on this extensive site. The house was a Georgian building, three storeys high, with a balustraded roof, and contained twenty-four rooms, including a panelled dining-room. For about twenty years it was the residence of Sir John McNeill of Colonsay who died in 1883. Among his guests was Florence Nightingale who stayed at the house on several occasions. Lord Gifford, the Scottish judge who inaugurated the Gifford Lectures on Religion and died in 1887, also lived here.

Unoccupied and likely to remain so by 1946, the mansion was taken over by Edinburgh Corporation who used it as emergency accommodation, and in 1953 twelve families had found refuge here. Unhappily, on 1st January the following year Granton House was almost completely gutted by fire, after which all hope of rebuilding it was given up.

The fate of Granton House is an all too familiar story, but a much stranger one can be told of a little dwelling of very different character in Granton. During the mid-1830s, when the Duke of Buccleuch was building Granton Harbour, the stone for its construction was brought from a quarry which had been opened a mile or more to the west at Granton Point beyond Granton Castle and Caroline Park. The quarry aroused widespread interest when a great fossil tree – an Araucaria 75 feet long – was discovered and had to be left *in situ* as it was too large and heavy to be removed. The overseer, Mr Robert Muir, lived in a house on the edge of the quarry with a powerful pumping engine in the basement which kept down the water level, and a little garden which he took great pride in cultivating. Twenty years later, as more and more stone was being won from the quarry, fears were expressed about its safety, and the men were given permission to work on the landward faces only. But anxieties were reinforced by a season of severe storms and winds. Confidence being restored, however, as the weather improved, the quarrymen slept soundly in their beds again – all except Robert Muir who awoke suddenly one night with a feeling of unease although no wind was blowing and no alarming sounds were to be heard. Looking up from his bed, he noticed a large crack in the ceiling above his head. As he watched the crack grew steadily wider and, with only a moment or two to spare, he roused his family and quickly hustled them outside. At the same moment the sea rushed in from the submerging quarry and half of the house disappeared beneath the water. When the men arrived for work in the morning, all they could see were planks of wood, wheelbarrows and bits of furniture floating in the Firth. Attempts were made to recover some valuable equipment but the cost proved to be too great and they were abandoned.

Some years after this near disaster, the first marine station for scientific research in Great Britain was built on the site at Granton Point and was opened on 15th April 1884 with its steam yacht and floating laboratory, the founder, as recorded in chapter 3, being Sir John Murray of Challenger Lodge.

Granton Point and, in particular, Granton House itself, are recalled in *Tales of a Great Grand-Aunt*, the recollections of Margaret Hope (1810–1893), an unmarried daughter of the Rt. Hon. Charles Hope (1763–1851) whose judicial title was Lord Granton, who held the office of Lord President of the Court of Session and who had married Charlotte, daughter of the second Earl of Hopetoun, which she wrote for her great grand-nieces and -nephews. Extracts from this otherwise unpublished work can be read in the January 1951 edition of *Blackwood's Magazine*. Writing in 1891 when she was over eighty years of age, she paints a vivid picture of the Point and of the Black Rocks below Granton House in her account of the visit of George IV in 1822 'when all of Scotland who could come to Edinburgh flocked to see a king'. After all, 'was not Charles II the last king here?'

Below Granton House with its woods there was only a hedge and a sunk fence and although, in 1891, the quarry 'with the sea let into it' was all that could be seen, at the time of the king's visit the area consisted of a grass field 'which came to a point on a level many feet above the sea', while underneath on the shore a ledge of rocks ran into the sea, the rocks and the land on the point forming a bay below Granton 'full and deep in high tide.' In low water, however, the sea ran out, leaving wet sands, as far as a ridge of rocks 'which we called the black rocks because they were all covered with mussels: and to those rocks, when our nurse gave us leave, with bare feet we ran across the wet sands to gather them'. Carrying the mussels home to Granton House they boiled them on the nursery fire, 'sitting on the floor and picking out and eating them as their shells opened with the heat'.

Her father had the ground on a 99-year lease from the Duke of Buccleuch and when he built Granton House in 1807, a house in which she herself was born, 'there was only a footpath along the beach from Cramond to Newhaven with a wall most of the way'.

On the evening before the king's arrival 'a very dense sea mist came up so that soon we could not see even the trees around the house. Of a sudden we were startled by loud cries of distress from the sea – louder and louder they came. Our father very soon concluded that one of the steamers that were so constantly bringing down people from Stirling to see His Majesty, had, in the fog, lost her way and got on to the Black Rocks opposite the house. James mounted a pony in haste to go to Cramond to see if a boat could be launched. Papa and his men hurried down to the shore. The tide was fast ebbing, so if only the people could have known, they were in no danger. This was shouted to them, and the promise that help was coming. As the tide went out my father made his way through the sea with his men until he reached the rocks and crossed to the steamer. The outside of the small reef is always under water, but the land side is quite bare when the tide is out.

'The passengers were in sad terror, and Papa had difficulty in persuading them that he had walked out to the ship and that, since the tide was still going out, they could all walk safely to land if they would trust to his guidance through the thick fog.' As the captain knew, the steamer would have to wait 'till the next tide came to its full height to float it off'. 'At last the people were persuaded to venture on to the rocks and over the wet sand, and Papa brought them all up to the house. Mama had been making every preparation to refresh them in the kitchen, which was soon crowded with still alarmed people. When the men passengers had been refreshed they set off with a guide to walk to Edinburgh: the women remained all night in the kitchen till morning gave them courage to follow the men. In the crowd Mama discovered a delicate lady with a very young infant. She our mother put into a comfortable bed, fed and soothed her to sleep, and took her up next day in the carriage to Edinburgh.

'George IV's visit to Edinburgh was an event of the nineteenth century which history has already written. Therefore, one who was then still a girl of twelve has little to say.' She only saw him once in the city when the king was entering it and 'we were standing on the steps of the Register House as the procession passed'. However, 'my recollection of His Majesty's departure from Edinburgh is very clear. On embarking, his fleet came up to Hopetoun House to pay a visit (the only private visit he made) to Lord Hopetoun, and it was expected to have been for him a brilliant farewell to Scotland. But alas! a day of very heavy rain and fierce east winds made Hopetoun House and all as gloomy as could be.

'Uncle Hopetoun and Lord Hope on horseback, with the County Yeomanry, met him on landing at St. Edgar's Pier, to conduct his carriage to the house. Hundreds had been invited, and were intended to have been entertained and to have seen His Majesty outside the house, but the rain was so very heavy that all had to be crushed within, to the Hall and into the small room not required for the royal visit. It had been intended that the Royal Archers would line the long steps from the carriage up to the front door, but instead they were inside the Hall, drawn up in lines from the outer door for His Majesty to pass between. That we children might be sure of seeing His Majesty, we were placed in front of the Archers.

'Now we knew the King was really coming, like some of my companions I was rather alarmed. We only knew kings in history and I supposed them far above other mortals. Almost as soon as Aunt had reached the door, it was thrown open, and His Majesty stepped in from the pouring rain to meet her. Then all my ideas were changed; for at once he seemed to pay all the homage to her and permit none from her. He led her into the crowded Hall and through the line of Archers as though he were leading in a royal lady to her subjects. They passed into the rooms and we saw them no more.'

Nevertheless, 'although I saw no more, I heard that His Majesty's courtly manner to my Aunt was the same all through the visit. When they went into the luncheon, he led her in and placed her in the chair of State that had been put there for himself and took a low seat by her. Before leaving the banquet, he asked to see her ten sons.' Nine were brought in, including the youngest who was only a year old. But where was Lord Houpetoun's eldest son? He could not be found, 'and only we young ones knew where he was. When it was near the time for the King's departure, we all ran up the south stair to watch from a window. Before us, however, we found that another had come, our eldest cousin. We heard the repeated cries of "Lord Hope, Lord Hope", but he never moved, and held us from doing so, fearing that his place of hiding would be discovered; for he knew why they were calling him. It was his shyness that kept him silent; for as soon as the horses appeared to escort His Majesty away, down he ran and was in his saddle ere his father and the others came out. I recollect no more of the day.'

In winter, when the trees were leafless, 'from our nursery window', in Granton House, 'we could see the Point and one day we children and our nurses saw two sailors rushing round the Point and towards our house. Then I heard of other men coming shortly afterwards to the house' and searching for the sailors; but they left some time later without finding them. Although at that tender age she did not fully understand what they were doing, she knew that this had been a visit from the dreaded Press Gang and that 'our old nurse had hid them safe till dark' when they were able to make their escape. (Perhaps one of their shipmates made it to the Trinity Mains Farmhouse bolthole.) She thought of this incident 'as a nursery mystery not to be mentioned.'

'Another terror in childhood' was on 'a night when I found out that at full tide and on moonlight nights smugglers came to these rocks in their boats. Of course I knew not what they were, but saw there was fear about them in the nursery. Therefore I was afraid and when, late at night, carts were heard going down a back road to the shore I have recollections, when I was supposed to be asleep, of hearing the maids say these were carts going down to meet the smugglers; and I once saw these terrible men, as I remember, one very stormy morning. From the nursery window we saw them on the shore (and they were also in our wood) and a boat on the shore. They had not been able to get away in time, and I think I heard there were barrels found hid in our wood', though she could not remember who had found them.

Happier memories were of the boats of the oyster dredgers. From the open windows of their schoolroom, on mild winter evenings, they listened to the men who 'always chanted some song which came floating to us through the darkness.' And then 'in summer, at full tide and near to sunset, two or three boats would come in just under the windows with nets to haul for salmon trout. We all gathered to see the setting sun's rays on the calm sea, the picturesque boats and nets and men, and then the lovely trout – such excitement as the nets were slowly hauled in! I doubt if there are any salmon trout to be caught there now' – in 1891.

Her father entertained largely in Granton House, 'both for Bench and still more for the Bar. These dinner-parties were always given on Fridays and Saturdays – of course only my two eldest sisters dined – but as soon as the dessert was on the table a bell was rung for us. There was a screen behind my father's chair and we had to go round it, with pleasure when there was no company, but only by a well-remembered effort of courage when we knew we had to come before perhaps twenty people. I remember being always glad when I found one particular gentleman by my mother; I used to put my stool near to him; for he had always some little story to

Granton House was destroyed by fire on 1st January 1954 when this picture was taken. At that time it was occupied by twelve families, all of whom were rescued, who had been given emergency accommodation here by Edinburgh Corporation. The roof, which had been retiled only two weeks before, had crashed to the ground and the remaining walls were then demolished.
(*Photograph courtesy Scotsman Publications Ltd.*)

tell me and kindly saw that the dessert plate on my knee was replenished. And when my mother rose and he did so too, I was sorry to see that he was lame. I did not ask his name then, but afterwards I knew him as Sir Walter Scott.'

'It was long before our time that beggars were of the dignity and importance or enjoyed all the privileges of an "Eddie Ochiltree", but they were still allowed to beg, if not by law, certainly by custom. Many came to Granton and were served there, and, as is said in *The Antiquary*, "the handful of meal was scarce denied by the poorest cottager". Often and often, when sitting in Peggy Morison's and other cottages, I have seen the handful of meal given even before it was asked for, to some poor man or woman.

'But there was still remaining another custom of begging that I have never seen in print. It was this: that when destitute persons without claim on the Parish were crippled and could not wander about to beg, they were carried from house to house – carried in barrows, a kind of long open box with handles at each end. And the unwritten law was that the barrow was carried from your own door and laid down at the door of the next house. And so the poor creature was lodged and fed through the country.

'I had personal knowledge of this, for one day such a barrow with a very distressed and crippled woman was laid down at Granton House door. I was surprised, but those of the house just said it was the custom. I think I must have been about ten years old. This poor woman had, on her way to Granton, been so teased by boys when passing along, that she was almost crazed, and in my mother's mind there was no thought of sending her on. So the barrow was lodged in the gardener's house. Now the next house she would have been carried to was Mr Dodd's farm, and then on to Caroline Park. So my mother and Mrs Cockburn took counsel together and decided that she must be kept and her wanderings ended. She was lodged in a cottage outside Caroline Park wall where only one woman lived, and her barrow was fitted up as a bed and placed so that from it she could look out of the window. Mary Hastie, the other woman, was to go daily to Caroline Park for dinner to serve for "Jenny" and for herself, and Mama was to supply all else required.

'This old Jenny had had an eventful history. She had gone with our army to Spain. I forget the regiment, but her husband and three sons in it had all been killed at the Battle of Corunna. She was in fever when the troops were due to come home, and with other sick patients and wounded soldiers was left in an hospital in Spain. She had no idea how long she was there, but, when the fever left her, her limbs were powerless, and she had become a cripple for life. In time, with other sick people, she was put aboard a ship and landed at Greenock, and had ever since, she knew not how long, been carried through the country. She said she was sure she had had a fourth son, almost a boy, in the regiment, and that he was not killed.

'As she was perfectly clear in all this account, my father took pains to ascertain if her history were true. From the Horse Guards and from the Colonel of the Regiment, he found that it was indeed correct about the battle and the loss of her husband and sons, and that her fourth son was still alive and a private in the same regiment. (A year or two later he got leave and came to visit her.)

'After she had recovered from all her wanderings and troubles she was shown to be a very intelligent woman, and she had many histories to tell us in our constant visits to her. As she could not stretch her legs to the end of her barrow, she gave the end of it to a hen, which had its nest there and laid its eggs there. She knitted stockings and read, and was ever ready for a chat. And when we went with her tea and anything else that was necessary, she was always proud to give us a fresh egg.'

'On the point of the field above the shore my father (by the Duke's leave) had a high flagstaff where a large Union Jack was hoisted on the King's birthday and on other great days.

My brother commanded a ship for three years on the North Sea and he often came in when my father invited the officers to dinner. His way of doing so was, of a morning, to hoist a white flag, namely a large dinner cloth, on this flagstaff!' When in full evening dress, Lord Granton wore black silk stockings with buckles at the knee and on his shoes, and a shirt 'with its front of broad cambric frill'.

In 1842, the year of Queen Victoria's first official visit to Scotland after her coronation, Margaret Hope (no longer resident at Granton) attended the Queen's 'Drawingroom' at Dalkeith Palace. 'As it was held at short notice and there was not time for making Court dresses, the Queen ordered "only evening full dress with flowers on the head and not feathers".'

In 1831 the family had moved out of Granton House and Miss Hope writes with feeling of the occasion. In September when the last day came 'and everything and everyone had departed for Edinburgh, my mother chose to remain for that night and chose me as the one to remain with her. She and I walked through the woods down to the Point and sat on the rocks. Well do I recollect that lovely day, the sea so calm, the views down the Firth to the Isle of May and up to the point at Dalmeny above the wood. The next day the last journey was made by the family coach from Granton to Edinburgh.'

Her mother died in January 1834 and her father, the builder of Granton House, in October 1851. Both are buried in the Mausoleum at Hopetoun House.

Round the corner from the foot of Granton Road, on high ground overlooking Granton Harbour, stands Lufra House. It was occupied by a shipping agent in 1860 but had much grander origins, having been built, exactly ten years earlier, by the Duke of Buccleuch as a yachting house with a yachtsman's cottage in the garden. The house has four bedrooms, and a laundry in the basement, and was called Lufra after the Duke's yacht which in turn had been called after one of Sir Walter Scott's dogs.

When Queen Victoria made her well-documented visit to Edinburgh in 1842 it is on record that arrangements were made for her to arrive in the Royal Yacht at Granton so that the Duke of Buccleuch, who had paid for it himself, could show off to her his fine new harbour! It had been partially opened, says James Grant, 'on the Queen's coronation day, 28th June 1838.'

On the opposite side of West Shore Road from the former Granton House another house of the same period but displaying a mixture of Georgian and neo-Gothic styles called Craigroyston can be seen beyond its surrounding trees and lawns, and it also is in the ownership of Scottish Gas, now British Gas Scotland. Its rooftop battlements resemble two square tower heads and it has an arched doorway in its entrance porch. The bay windows were inserted later, and additions and considerable internal alterations were made by Sir Robert Lorimer in 1907–8. Craigroyston House was in use as a Naval Headquarters during the war.

In 1776 William Davidson, having in the best tradition of Scottish merchants spent many years trading in Rotterdam, amassing by his industry sufficient wealth to purchase an estate, acquired the barony of Muirhouse close to the shore above the Cramond Esplanade. The original house built here for himself and his family was replaced in 1832 by the present conspicuous mansion in Marine Drive, still known as Muirhouse. A square tower rises above this asymmetrical, two-storeyed, ecclesiastically-windowed Tudor pile with chimneys like tall pinnacles, and interesting features of the interior are the frescoes painted by Zephaniah Bell in the drawing-room when the house was rebuilt in 1832. Muirhouse is an A-listed building and has served as office premises for commercial enterprise in recent years.

The founding family gave its name to Davidson's Mains, and it was from them that Randall Thomas Davidson (born at No. 15 Inverleith Place in 1848), Chaplain to Queen Victoria in 1878 and Archbishop of Canterbury from 1903 to

Muirhouse, a conspicuous seaside mansion built by the
Davidsons of Davidson's Mains in 1832.

1928, was descended. As Archbishop of Canterbury he
crowned King George V in 1911.

The older building called Muirhouse had been a royal hunting lodge and below it the steep, wooded banks down to the
shore were only divided from the Granton wood by a ditch
very easily, said Margaret Hope, and very frequently jumped
across!

A short distance to the west, the Victorian house once
known as Broomfield overlooks the water and its stone-strewn
shoreline beyond trees and the grass banks on which it
stands. Built in the mid-19th century, it belonged to an aunt
of the same Earl Haig who gave his name to the World War I

Ex-Servicemen's Settlement in Trinity. Broomfield was suggested as a suitable clubhouse for a golf course which was under consideration in 1938, but the whole scheme was abandoned and the course was never laid out. The grey stone house, with its prominent chimneys and many gables, is now better known as the Commodore Hotel and has a large modern extension to the east.

The foreshore here is rich in fossil-bearing carboniferous rocks as old as 340 million years. In contrast to the giant araucaria laid bare at Granton Point, a gap in the fossil records was filled when tiny fossilised eel-like marine creatures were found at Muirhouse, the first in 1925 which remained unidentified until 1984 when further exploration among the rocks was made and revealed at least three others, thus ending a search by geologists which had lasted for well over a hundred years. Although other similar fossils were known to exist in different parts of the world, these were the first complete examples to be discovered and are considered to be of major importance in this field of study.

Since the early years when the first developers sank their taproots in the virgin soil of the coastal belt, and farmed and fished and traded and raised substantial houses for themselves and their descendants, later and more numerous roots have been put down as well, and serried rows of suburban flats and villas have spread out across the Wardie Muir, their numbers increasing with the passing years. To conserve the ancient places beside the new is to ensure a continuity of history – a history in stone – a heritage of houses.

Index